YOU

ARE

WHAT

YOU

WORSHIP

How true worship shapes us into the people
we were made to be

JONATHAN AZZARELLO

ACKNOWLEDGEMENTS

This book could not and would not have ever happened without the amazing people in my life. To my amazing wife Rachel, thank you for your incredible support, encouragement, and patience as I wrote this book. To my dear friend Matt, thank you for your friendship, wisdom, and countless hours of discussing the topics of this book with me. To my friend Alex, thank you for your theological insight and feedback during the editing process. To my sister Kellie, thank you for proofreading and for your encouragement. To my lead pastor Andrew, thank you for pointing my family and me to Jesus by faithfully preaching the Word each week.

CONTENTS

INTRODUCTION

A few years ago, my good friend Matt and I began studying the Bible together in a way that I had never really done before. We took our time reading one or two chapters per week so we could wrap our minds around what was happening through each passage of Scripture. We wanted to know the historical and theological context; so we read commentaries, ancient maps, articles, and any other resources we could find along the way. We would each journal a summary of the chapter we read, along with anything specific that we had learned, and then we would send a copy of our journals to each other.

As disciplined as I'd like to think that I am, studying the Bible is one of the easiest appointments on my calendar to cancel. But doing it with a friend kept me honest and motivated. I can honestly say that this journey has been life-changing for me. In fact, studying the Bible in this way caused the major paradigm shift in my life that led me to write this book.

As I studied the Bible, it felt like I had a backstage pass to God's big show. I have read through it before, but this time it was different. I read it with fresh eyes and a new passion to know God more. And I feel that I do. I learned more about his likes and dislikes; what angered him and what pleased him. And what I couldn't get over (and still can't) is the stark contrast between worship in the Bible and worship as we know it. Worship as we know it has been reduced to singing in church, listening to podcasts, and going to a mid-week Bible study. Don't get me wrong — these things are important. But *biblical* worship is so much more than this. Biblical worship is an admiration that leads to a transformation. It is not only a passion to be with God, but also a passion to be transformed by God into the image he designed us to reflect. God's profound desire for humanity is that we embody his relational qualities in all of our relationships. God's passion is for us to bear his image by loving him and loving people. This is an emphasis in the Bible that, I believe, is not an emphasis in modern Christianity. There is a clarity in the Scriptures regarding humanity's purpose that seems to be unclear to many people today. As a worship pastor, I have a passion to see people worship in the fullest, most biblical sense of the word, not just in a song. And it's out of this passion to see people worship and out of the realization that many "Christians" are missing the mark in biblical worship that I felt prompted to write this book. This book is not about music or congregational singing, though I will address both topics. This book is about true worship. It's about the kind of worship that shapes every part of us into who we are and what we do.

In the early 1930s, American nutritionist Victor Lindlahr coined the phrase and later published a book called, "You Are What You Eat." Lindlahr took cues from the French lawyer Anthelme Brillat-Savarin who wrote in 1826, "Tell me what you eat, and I will tell you what you are." The idea was that whatever you put into your belly would determine the condition of your mental and physical health. In other words—junk in, junk out. If you eat healthy, then you will be healthy. This concept is not only true metabolically, but also spiritually.

Worship shapes us, and we can tell what we worship by the way that we live our lives. This book is about how the characteristics, values, and actions that we personify tell the story of what we are worshiping. What we are filled with is what will flow out of us, and what we love will determine how we live.

"You will recognize them by their fruits. Are grapes gathered from thorn bushes, or figs from thistles? Likewise, every good tree bears good fruit." — Matthew 7:16-17 (NIV)

I never dreamed in a million years that I would write a book, and I've never had a desire to before this year. But like the prophet Jeremiah, this message that God planted into my heart felt like a burning fire shut up in my bones, and it had to come out. My goal is to expose the essence of the true, life-changing, biblical worship that God desires from us, and then to call us into it.

3

This book is divided into four parts. Part one — Origin of Worship — lays the groundwork for the design and purpose of humanity and shows the role that worship plays in the process of becoming who we are. This part is foundational for understanding the rest of the book. If you've grown up around church, then chapters two and three may feel laborious, but stick with it. It sets the stage for part two — Product of Worship — which is really where the heart of the book begins. This part digs into the identity and purpose of a true worshiper. It paints a practical picture of what it looks like to be hidden in Jesus. The point of this section is not to guilt you into doing more or trying harder, but to help you understand the path that God wants for your life and how to walk on it. Part three — Transformed by Worship — unpacks the concept of transformational worship, giving practical tools for fueling a life of worship, along with ways to test the authenticity of your faith. The last part — Every Day, Worship — dives into what a lifestyle of worship looks like every day of the week. Worship isn't just a Sunday thing; it's an everyday thing. It covers topics like work, rest, and the purpose of church gatherings.

I pray that as you read this book you will allow it to challenge your priorities, your purpose, and the way you think about worship. I hope you will take your time with it. Wrestle with it, meditate on it, and discuss it with a friend. So here we go. You are what you worship.

PART 1
ORIGIN OF WORSHIP

CHAPTER 1

THE WAY YOU WERE MADE

It was Easter morning, seconds before church was about to start, as I flung my guitar strap over my shoulder and prepared to step up to the microphone. I'd been the worship pastor at our church for seven years. Typically, Easter Sunday is like the Super Bowl of all church services. It's fun, full of energy, and everyone is ready to go nuts about Jesus. But this time something was different for me. The feelings of excitement and anticipation were missing. There were no butterflies in my stomach—no nerves. My emotions were numb. Maybe this is the way Tom Brady felt as he was entering the field for his ninth Super Bowl appearance.

As the stage lights came up and the house lights went down, I set my mental switch to autopilot and stepped up to the microphone, "Welcome, church. Jesus is alive! Let's stand and worship."

I knew before the service began that there would be some people in the room who were enthusiastic, ready to sing. Others would be there because they were being a good friend to whoever had invited them. And others would be there because that's just what Christians do, especially on Easter Sunday. As I began singing and strumming my guitar, I couldn't help but notice the guy on the third row, sipping his cup of coffee, looking around as if he were people-watching at the mall. Two friends in the back of the room who hadn't seen each other in a week were embracing each other, sharing a laugh over the sound of the band. The room was filled with people who were all spiritually and emotionally in different places, ranging from complete indifference to genuine contemplation (and everything in between). Though I was standing on the stage, it felt like I was hovering above the room. I was there — but not there. It was truly an out-of-body experience.

Here I was in my early thirties at a lower-end of the spectrum mega-church, playing my guitar, singing my songs, and smacking everyone's proverbial balloon back up in the air so they could get through the week — only to come back a week later and do it again. I knew as a worship leader that I was helping to shape hearts and minds for Jesus, but all I could think in this moment was, "What mold am I actually shaping hearts into?"

Flash back two weeks earlier. I had just returned home from a mission's trip to Milan, Italy. I had been planning to do missions work in Italy since I was ten years old; so, I had invested a lot of emotional stock in this week-long trip. Milan is home to the third-largest Roman cathedral in all of Europe, yet it is overshadowed by the fashion industry and a lifestyle known to the Italians as the "Bella

Figura," which translated into English means, "Beautiful Figure." This lifestyle is built on keeping up appearances and making good impressions. It's about portraying the image by which you'd like to be seen. Every day, designer handbags, trendy coats, and expensive watches fill the fashion square of the "Quadrilatero della moda." The lifestyle of Europe's fashion capital is as much a facade as the religious monuments and cathedrals that line the city. There is an age-defying, surface-level image of beauty that everyone is chasing, but it's an image that makes promises it can never keep. It tells you that the more you have, the more content you will be. But this is never the case.

The need to "show your best face" is not unique to the Bella Figura. This same mindset has overtaken social media accounts and social circles all over the world. Even modern Christianity has a face for what success looks like. You can see it on an Instagram post with a cup of coffee, Bible verse calligraphy, and an ESV Study Bible. It has a church bumper sticker on the back of a Yukon (I have my church bumper sticker on the back of my Yukon). There is an external image that says, "I have my life together." And this is the image I was portraying as I stood center-stage, dawning the persona of the quintessential worship leader (skinny jeans and all). I'd never really been one to crave the spotlight, but there was a certain sense of pride that I had in my own self-image. However, my self-image never felt emptier than it did that Easter morning. When I was younger, I felt like God was going to do something extraordinary through me. I had ambitions and idealistic dreams of doing something great, but what did that even mean anymore? Everything I was doing with my life felt so small and insignificant, even though I didn't believe that it was. Maybe I was tired or overworked. Maybe I was depressed. Maybe the mission's trip backfired. Perhaps it did.

In all my years of ministry, I've always enjoyed leading worship and working at a church. But at that moment, more than ever, it felt like something essential was missing. Something very real was lacking. Even in my most authentic moments, I felt disingenuous and incomplete. I started questioning the validity and spiritual significance of what I was doing with my life. I lead people to sing lyrics like, "Praise is a weapon," and "Hallelujah! You have won it all for me," but it seemed like so many people who were singing these songs were losing battles left and right. Our songs touted victory and praise, but deep-down people were feeling defeat and shame.

My mind was racing a thousand miles per hour, and everything else around me was moving in slow motion. "Shouldn't our worship lead to something more than just a song?" I thought to myself. "We come to church, we sing our songs, we take our notes, and then we go back to living our lives the way we came. Are we living out the same 'Bella Figura' lifestyle with a Christian label on it? Is this truly the image we are meant to bear? Is this the worship God desires? Is there something more, something bigger?" I've asked similar questions before, but never with as much conviction and desperation.

The word "worship" was in my job title. I eat, sleep, and breathe all things worship. I've read books on it, researched it, and led people into it, but something about our understanding of worship seemed anemic. We might understand that worship involves sacrifice, but we've cheapened the definition of sacrifice. We call it sacrifice when we drop a twenty in the offering plate or when we sing in front of people even when we don't feel like it.

As a worship leader, I knew I was called to do more than just lead people in a five-minute song. I was called to lead people into a much deeper song—one that sings the melody of purpose and passion with our whole life. The purpose of worship and the ultimate purpose of humanity are more intrinsically connected than we might even know. Worship is the desire and passion for that which brings us purpose. And, I believe, from a relentless pursuit of seeking out in the Scriptures what genuine worship truly looks like, there is a paradigm-shifting purpose that each of us is called to that is infinitely greater than the one we might be settling for. There is a greater, more authentic image that we are called to embody that is different from the one we might currently be pursuing.

Most Christians clearly understand that we exist for God's glory, but how that plays out in everyday life is less clear. Giving God glory is not about pounding your chest and pointing to the sky as if celebrating a touchdown. It's about recognizing God's design for your life and living in it. In order to fully understand our purpose, we need to have a better understanding of humanity's design. After all, the success of any created thing is defined by its ability to fulfill the functions for which it was designed. We innately understand that things were made to be a certain way. In the book *Mere Christianity*, C.S. Lewis said, "The very idea of something being imperfect, of its not being what it ought to be, has certain consequences." In other words, when we see the destruction of a forest that was caused by a fire or a town that was decimated by a tornado, we know that it was not meant to be this way. When we see the pain and the brokenness of a person that was caused by the abuse of someone else, we feel at the core of our souls that this is not the way it should be. And in recognizing that things are not as they should be, we implicitly state that there is a certain way that things ought to be. The Maker of the universe created humanity to function in a certain way. There is a way in which we can look at all of life and humanity and say, "This is the way it should be."

People have chased everything under the sun from money to sex hoping to satisfy this desire for fullness and purpose, but it is in chasing after our hopes and dreams that often brings us to the moments where we cry out, "This is not how it should be."

Everything has a proper design that determines its purpose. For example, a hammer was designed to drive a nail into softer materials such as wood or drywall. If you were to measure the success of a hammer by how well it could cut through wood or remove screws, then the hammer would prove to be unsuccessful. The hammer might attempt to defy its design by trying to function as a screwdriver, but this does not change the fact that the hammer was not designed to be anything other than a hammer. Therefore, the hammer is most successful when it is being used to drive nails. That's when the hammer's true purpose is fulfilled. It's not the desire of the creation that defines its purpose or success, but rather the desire of the creator that establishes these things.

The same is true for humanity. As created beings, we, too, have been written into a specific design. We all have the same basic biological construct and genome, and we all share a common purpose that defines our success as humans. Though we control our decisions and our actions, we do not own the blueprint for our design. And because our desires do not innately align with our design, we often choose what we want rather than what we need as if we were able to define our own purpose. This logic follows one similar to entering a race without knowing where the finish line would be. If this were to happen, everyone would be running as fast as they could in different directions, as though they were choosing their own finish line, resulting in utter chaos. But this is not the way it all works.

You might be driven by the desire to climb a corporate ladder, achieve a marital status, sustain a lifestyle of comfort, or make a name for yourself; but maybe the pursuit of true happiness and the definition of success are not found in any of these things at all. Living within the bounds of our design is the only place that we can find our true purpose and freedom. In other words, we are most human when we function in the way that we were designed to function. And the Designer of humanity is none other than God himself. He is most glorified through us when we fulfill his purpose for us.

(#1) To best understand our purpose, we need to consider how we were designed. If we look at the Scriptures, we will find that we were designed to be image-reflectors and fruit-bearers. And the way that we conform to an image and produce fruit is through worship. Worship determines which image we reflect and what kind of fruit we bear. I want to break down who we were designed to be, what we were designed to do, and how we become these things.

Image-Reflector

"So, God created mankind in his own image, in the image of God he created them; male and female he created them." – Genesis 1:27 (NIV)

In May 1922, on the western end of the National Mall in Washington, D.C., the Lincoln Memorial was dedicated in honor of the nation's sixteenth president. After four years of constructing the nineteen-foot-tall statue, this marble image of Abraham Lincoln stands as a reminder of not only what he looked like but also the ideologies for which he stood. As the president who issued the Emancipation Proclamation in 1863, his memorial grounds would eventually become a significant venue for the Civil Rights Movement that took place one hundred years later. In August 1963, on the grounds of the Lincoln Memorial, Martin Luther King Jr. delivered his famous "I Have a Dream" speech; which touched hearts and lives in a way that affected people all over the world. The statue of President Lincoln still serves today as an image of equality and a reminder that "every man has a right to be equal with every other man." The statue of Abraham Lincoln was made to serve as a landmark of freedom and human value for every American life. This statue is an image that reflects his physical appearance as well as his policies and principles.

In a similar way, the greatest Artist of all time designed and formed Adam, the first human, to be an image that reflected himself; not only in appearance but also in virtue. The God of the universe made human beings to be a projection of his own holiness—to be physical representations of his relational qualities. He made the mountains to display his majesty, the oceans to tell of his vastness, and he made humans to exhibit his mercy and goodness. God created humanity in his own image, both male and female, to be demonstrations of his character—to be gracious, slow to anger, and full of love.

"For we are God's handiwork, created in Christ Jesus to do good works, which God prepared in advance for us to do." – *Ephesians 2:10 (NIV)*

As creatures made in the image of God, human beings hold intrinsic value. Regardless of age, race, gender, or stature, humans were crowned with glory and honor by the Lord of all creation to be reflectors of his own image.

> *"Yet you have made him a little lower than the heavenly beings and crowned him with glory and honor." — Psalm 8:5 (ESV)*

Fruit-bearer

If we look at the creation account in Genesis, we see that the Maker of the universe created humanity on the last day of creation, and his first documented words to them were, "Be fruitful and multiply" (Genesis 1:28).

To accurately discern the meaning of God's command to "Be fruitful and multiply," we need to consider that people were made as physical and spiritual beings. We are not strictly physical or spiritual; we are both. This means that everything we do has both physical and spiritual implications. Whether we are eating, drinking, thinking, or singing, we are always functioning within two dimensions because we are multi-dimensional beings. This is important to understand, especially before attempting to unpack God's first words to humanity. It may seem at face value that this was only a physical directive to simply make babies that make babies, but offspring are not the only fruit that humans produce. Though it may have been mostly a physical fruitfulness that God was referring to in Genesis, it is no coincidence that he chose these words. "Be fruitful and multiply" is a holistic imperative that speaks more to the design and purpose of humanity than it does to a moment of intimacy. ❧

So, what does it mean for a human to be fruitful? To determine if something is fruitful or not, we need to understand what that thing was designed to produce. For example, for an apple tree to be fruitful, it would need to produce apples, because that's what apple trees were designed to do. We would not measure the fruitfulness of an apple tree by how many bananas it produced because it was not designed to produce bananas. We could only determine the fruitfulness of an apple tree by how many apples it produced. There would be nothing more disappointing for an apple tree owner than having an apple tree that didn't produce apples. If you've ever planted a single apple tree in your yard, you may have experienced a fruitless tree. Apple trees require a companion tree for cross-pollination, and if there is no other apple tree within close proximity, the apple tree will not produce apples.

And so it is with humans. If humans were designed to be image-bearers of God, then fruitfulness would be the fullest, most complete manifestation of God's image. Fruitfulness would be the presence and embodiment of his relational characteristics and values, and if we live our lives without bearing this fruit, then we are no different from an apple tree with no apples. Physical fruitfulness and spiritual fruitfulness are produced in two different ways. Yes, the physical part of "Be fruitful and multiply" involves the reproductive system, but there is a spiritual reality of fruit-bearing that is much greater and has to do with our words, actions, and relationships. The reason I say it is greater is that things that are seen are temporal, but things that are unseen are eternal.

"So we fix our eyes not on what is seen, but on what is unseen, since what is seen is temporary, but what is unseen is eternal." – 2 Corinthians 4:18 (NIV)

The physical and spiritual are both important and directly impact each other. However, the physical will be outlasted by the spiritual. Physical fruit is a harbinger to a fuller meaning of the spiritual fruit that we are all called to bear. We are to fill the earth not just with physical fruit but also with spiritual fruit. This is what we were designed to do. The words that God spoke to Adam in the Garden of Eden would later be brought to a fuller meaning when Jesus would call his followers to bear fruit that lasts – the fruit of loving each other.

"You did not choose me, but I chose you and appointed you so that you might go and bear fruit – fruit that will last – and so that whatever you ask in my name the Father will give you. This is my command: Love each other." – John 15:16-17 (NIV)

Worshiper

A few years ago, I took my family to the Dixie Classic Fair in our hometown Winston-Salem. Tensions were running high after rescuing my son from the semi-traumatic experience of being bitten by a donkey in the petting zoo. We weren't supposed to pet the donkey, but we learned that the hard way. As we exited the petting zoo area, we turned the corner and saw a large crowd gathered around a performer of some kind; so, we walked over to get a closer look. It was a blacksmith. The crowd was mesmerized by his performance to simply shape tools and weapons out of steel. There was something enchanting about watching this artisan take the glowing orange steel from the 2500-degree forge and mold it into various shapes. Sparks shot out like fireworks as the hammer struck the steel that was being formed with ease as if it were putty. We watched this process for about twenty minutes; although I would have been content to stand there and watch him work for hours. In a similar way, God is like the great blacksmith who desires to take us through the fire like a piece of steel, forging us into the image he designed us to be. Though some may desire a destiny that is different from what God intended for us, he loves us too much to let us rust away in our futility.

As image-bearers of the living God, humans were innately designed to be pictures of God himself. We were designed to conform to his mold and represent his character by bearing the fruit of love. The process in which this molding and conforming happen is called "worship." Worship is desiring something so much that you long to be transformed by it. All humans are instinctively designed with the desire to be molded into something. We are all designed to worship. As food shapes our waistline, so our worship shapes the image that we bear. Since we were designed to bear the image of God, and since worship is the way by which we are transformed, it is no surprise that God's intention was that we become like him by worshiping him. Although the modern understanding of "worship" has been reduced to singing songs on Sunday morning, "worship" has a much deeper meaning. Here are some of my favorite definitions of what worship is:

WoW *"Worship is the submission of all our nature to God. It is the quickening of conscience by His holiness; the nourishment of mind with His truth; the purifying of imagination by His beauty; the opening of the heart to His love; the surrender of will to His purpose — and all of this gathered up in adoration, the most selfless emotion of which our nature is capable and therefore the chief remedy for that self-centeredness which is our original sin and the source of all actual sin." — William Temple*

"Worship is acknowledging that someone or something else is greater — worth more — and by consequence, to be obeyed, feared, and adored... Worship is the sign that in giving myself completely to someone or something, I want to be mastered by it." — Harold Best ○

Simply put, worship is the relentless pursuit of the heart's ultimate desire. It is chasing after something you value more than everything else. It's not just about what you do on Sunday mornings, but what drives your ambitions, passions, actions, and the trajectory of your entire life. Worship is more than a feeling or a checklist of things to do;

19

it's about beholding and becoming. It is the agreement of your soul with something other than yourself. It beholds an image and then conforms to it. Like a canvas that sits on an easel at the park and desires to be transformed by the artist, worship is the desire and pursuit of bringing joy to the artist by becoming his masterpiece.

Worship is never initiated; it is always a response to a grand revelation. We were created for beholding and responding. For example, when we behold a beautiful sunset, we might respond by taking a moment to admire its beauty and splendor. The feeling of admiration does not precede the vision of the sunset; it is a response to it. When we behold something on a greater scale, like the Grand Canyon, then our response will be even greater. We might take it in for a longer time, feeling it more deeply. Our hearts are always seeking an ultimate revelation that is worthy of our worship, and when we find it, we are happy to give ourselves over to it and be transformed by it. When we behold someone or something that, we believe, will give us purpose or pleasure, it captures our desires, passions, and thoughts; and it controls our words, decisions, and our pocketbooks. Our worship is awarded to the greatest, most ultimate vision that captures the gaze of our hearts.

We are designed to be relentless pursuers. We do not all worship the God of the Bible, but we all worship something. There is a throne on our hearts that we happily offer to one ultimate lord in our life. We love and pursue that one thing. We want to be mastered by it. This ultimate thing in our life captures our heart's eye. We obey it. We follow it.

We give ourselves over to it, and we are transformed by it. This is worship. Although true worship happens when the throne of our heart is occupied by the Living God, false worship (idolatry) happens when anything other than God fills that ultimate spot. When our heart's gaze is misdirected at things such as money, status, self-image, sex, relationships, houses, or cars, then we become deformed versions of the image we were designed to reflect.

"Above all, guard your heart, for everything you do flows from it." — Proverbs 4:23 (NIV)

Though worship manifests itself through our image and actions, it begins in the heart. The heart is the retina that captures the image of our worship. When our hearts see something worthy of our lives, we respond by giving our lives over to it. The heart is where the seed of worship takes root and works its way into our words, actions, and resources. We don't just roll the dice and choose something or someone to worship at random. We choose what we will worship as a response to an ultimate vision—one that we believe will fill the desire and insatiable hunger in our souls—even if that vision is blurred or inaccurate. For example, the worship of wealth might stem from a vision of money being the answer to all of our problems. The worship of sex or relationship status might come from a vision of intimacy filling our desire to be known and loved. Whatever image is burnt into our hearts is given the power to mold us and shape us. But there is only one mold that we were made

21

to fill, and there is only one God we were made to worship. Only when we worship him can we be truly satisfied; because only when we worship him can we be formed into the perfect image he designed us to reflect.

If you were to take a triangle-shaped peg and place it into a round hole, it would not fill the hole. The triangle peg might be able to fit inside the round hole, but it can never fill the hole entirely because it is the wrong shape. There will always be gaps. People are the same way. We were made in the shape of God; so, it should come as no surprise that God is the only thing that can truly fill us. Pursuing some other thing to satisfy the desires of our heart is like trying to fill a round hole with a triangle peg. Its efforts will always leave us wanting.

"Nothing will satisfy man but God, in whose image he was made." – Charles Spurgeon

As worship shapes us, it manifests into fruitfulness. Think about the design of a plant. A plant is made to produce fruit. It relentlessly chases after what will give it life and energy. A plant will contort its own body to grow towards the direction of the sun so that it can absorb the maximum amount of its energy. And the roots do the same thing underground as they pursue any semblance of water. When the plant drinks in from the water underground, it can begin to produce the fruit it was designed to produce. But if a plant lacks the energy from the sun and drinks from the dry, waterless soil, it will become just like the source from which it drank—dry and lifeless. In this metaphor, our hearts are like the root system. God's Word is water, and his love is the sun (Psalm 1). The thing that makes us alive is the same thing that produces the fruit which comes out of us. Beholding shapes our worship, and worship shapes us.

We are what we worship. The same is true for false worship (idolatry). The prophet Jeremiah told idolaters that they would become like the lifeless idols they worshiped, with eyes that can't see and ears that can't hear (Jeremiah 10:14). But when we worship the Author of life, we are made alive. When we worship the God of love, we are filled with love. Worship and fruitfulness are so intrinsically connected that you don't need to look very far to see what you are worshiping. Simply take inventory of your fruit and it will expose what you worship.

I believe the problem and the missing piece to our worship today is that Christians desire to worship God without being transformed by him. We've mastered the art of worshiping without consequence. We desire to be used by the Artist, but we deny his paint from absorbing into the canvas of our souls. We want to behold without becoming, but we must not fool ourselves into believing that worship can be one without the other. Worship changes us, and when our worship is fixed on our Maker, we will be transformed into the image we were designed to bear. We were made for worship, but there is just one problem—an enormous problem.

CHAPTER 2

THE WAY YOU ARE

Before any of us drew our first breath in this life, our worship was already completely broken. We are not the first generation of worshipers to miss the mark. Worship has been broken since the very beginning. For those who desire to worship God but have reservations about going all in, and for those who are not yet convinced of their need to worship with anything more than their Sunday mornings—this chapter serves as a call for us to see just how desperately we need God. Before we can ever worship God rightly, we must understand what he has done to deserve our devotion. And in order to do that, we must first understand the reality of our brokenness. In this chapter, I will unpack what led to the cause of our fallen condition and the implications of our broken worship. To understand how we can live out our purpose of reflecting God's image, we must first understand our plight. Imagine being lost in the middle of a jungle. A map would only be helpful if you were first able to identify where you were. This chapter serves as the little star on a map that says, "You are here."

24

Broken Worship

In Genesis 3, after God created man and woman, he laid out some family rules for them to follow. These rules were not given to deprive them of anything other than grief and sorrow. They were for their protection—for their freedom. As Tim Keller said, "In many areas of life, freedom is not so much the absence of restrictions as finding the right ones, the liberating restrictions." God outlined the boundaries of their freedom with his Word. His commands were life, and to step outside of them would be—well—death. The Father lovingly told them they could eat from any tree in the entire garden except for the tree in the middle— the Tree of Knowledge of Good and Evil. God forbade them to eat from this one tree.

No problem, right? Adam and Eve were literally in paradise; but deception slithered into the garden in the form of a serpent, telling Eve that greater power and fulfillment were on the other side of God's boundary lines. The serpent told Eve that God only forbade them to eat from this tree because he was threatened by what would happen if they did. The serpent told her that if they ate of the fruit that they would become like gods. Though it may seem at first that the serpent was entirely at fault for tricking Eve into believing such a lie, Eve's problem first started in her own heart. You see, God gave them purpose and meaning. As long as they worshiped God, they reflected his image. As long as they reflected his image, they were living within the parameters of their design. They were living their best life.

They were filled with joy and had everything they would ever need. But the idea that she could be just as powerful as God was a temptation that captured the gaze of her heart. At that moment, pride became the gardening shears that severed the root of worship. She became like a rose that was detached from the vine. Though she and Adam appeared to be alive, they had lost all ability to bear the kind of fruit that remains, because they had been cut-off from their life-source — God. The moment she kicked God off the throne of her heart, her image became distorted. Adam and Eve were supposed to have dominion over all the animals, but they allowed an animal to have dominion over them.

The first thing that broke was her worship, and everything went downhill from there. Becoming a god looked like a dream worth chasing, but this dream quickly turned into a nightmare. Adam and Eve sinned against God and were immediately burdened by their shame. They were like mirrors that once reflected God's perfect image but had now been shattered into a million pieces. The damage had been done, and it was irreparable. They hid from God because they knew that they were reflecting a deformed image. They had cheated on him, and now they had to leave the garden. God cursed the very ground they walked on, and Adam's seed was spoiled for generations to come. Every seed of Adam, no matter how good it appeared to be, was flawed. None of his descendants would function correctly because they were all cut from the same defective cloth. Though Adam had once been fruitful, his fruit was now rotten. Though he once reflected the image of God, his image was now twisted. Though he once walked in his purpose, his purpose was confounded. Adam's children would become angry, envious, murderous thieves. It only took one sin to contaminate the entire bloodstream of humanity. One act of idolatry broke the worship for each generation to come.

Let me illustrate.

If I were to take a clean glass from the kitchen cabinet, fill it with ice-cold, purified, drinking water, and hand it to you on a hot, summer day, you would probably drink it. But if I were to take that same glass of water and add to it the tiniest piece of excrement from a large animal, this would undoubtedly be a game-changer. Would you drink even one sip from this glass, or would you consider the entire glass to be undrinkable? Just the thought of taking a sip would be repulsive (though this illustration is still less egregious than its antecedent). Even though the glass of water only had one blemish, it was enough to render the entire glass undrinkable. Not only would this water be undrinkable, but it would also need to be poured out behind a tree somewhere far away from the house, for it would be too unclean to be poured down the kitchen drain. This is how one sin has affected all of humanity. The water has been polluted — all of it.

"Therefore, just as sin came into the world through one man, and death through sin, and so death spread to all men because all sinned." — Romans 5:12 (ESV)

Each of us starts this journey of life reflecting the broken image of Adam. Though we may look alive on the outside, we are totally depraved under the hood. Our worship wires are crossed. Our desires are confused like a broken compass. Adam and Eve disobeyed God because they thought that they would become greater than God. Do we not reflect Adam and Eve every time we cut corners to get ahead? We don't need to be taught how to be dishonest or how to lie; it all comes too naturally. We don't long to worship the Father and reflect his image anymore. Everything was flipped upside down. And we get this from our great, great, great, (many more greats) grandfather — Adam.

I have three boys under the age of seven. You can probably guess what would happen if I were to put one toy monster truck in a room with all three of them. They would fight. They would argue about who should get the toy. They would sooner destroy the toy than concede it to be enjoyed by their brothers. I didn't have to teach them to be selfish; it flows naturally from who they are. The desires of our hearts are broken, and these broken desires lead to a life of broken worship.

"For out of the heart come evil thoughts, murder, adultery, sexual immorality, theft, false witness, slander." – Matthew 15:19 *(ESV)*

Lifeless

As a dad of six children who always seem to be hungry, most of which are in a state of constant snacking, I discovered that having a garden could save us money. I have done the whole gardening thing before in small doses, but this year we went all out. I planted six rows of fruits and vegetables — each row being over thirty feet long. There is nothing more cathartic than working in the garden during the lovely spring weather, watching the seedlings break through the soil and begin to blossom, as I impatiently waited to reap the harvest. I have learned that gardening in the springtime is infinitely more enjoyable than gardening in the humid summers of North Carolina. However enjoyable or unenjoyable it may have been at times, I was committed to having a successful garden. I had moved past the point of being a just-for-leisure gardener. I was doing it for the practicality of having an ample supply of vegetables for the minimal cost of a few packs of seeds (we won't talk about the countless hours of hard, manual labor, of course).

I have learned over the years that one key to having a successful garden is to remove all the obstacles such as pests and weeds. We had our fair share of pests from birds to squash beetles, but the pests I spent the most time removing were the weeds. I knew that if I didn't pull weeds every few days, they would overtake the garden and that would be the end of it. So, I spent a good amount of time each morning in the garden pulling weeds and pruning the plants. I watched YouTube videos and read a plethora of articles on best practices for pruning the various plants in our garden. One thing I learned was that it was necessary to prune some of the lower leaves of our zucchini and squash plants, especially the sickly-looking leaves, to allow for more direct sunlight; so, I did.

One day, as I was pulling the weeds and thinning out some of the lower leaves of the squash plants, I noticed that one of our squash plants wasn't looking so great. I thought I'd give it some extra TLC to nurse it back to health. As I grabbed on to one of the shriveled, brown leaves towards the bottom of the plant, I gave it a gentle tug upward. As I pulled the leaf, to my astonishment, I managed to pull the entire plant out of the ground. I was stunned. Apparently, the plant was in worse condition than I had even realized. It didn't take much effort at all to completely detach the plant from the root just above the soil's surface. The plant was large and already had a few squashes on it, but sadly this plant's life had come to an abrupt end. Though it still had vegetables attached to it and appeared to be in decent condition, it would never "bear fruit" again. It was dead. The squash plant was not only done producing, but it would also eventually shrivel up and rot in our compost pile.

The way that humanity detached from the Father in the garden was much like my squash plant being detached from its roots. Adam and Eve appeared to be alive, but they had been cut off from their life-source. They were no longer capable of bearing the fruit they were intended to bear (Romans 6:20-21). "Be fruitful and multiply" was not something that was within their power of doing. No amount of care or nurturing could cause them to produce the fruit they were created to bear because they were spiritually dead — like the squash plant.

However, Adam and Eve were not the only broken images. Generation after generation of broken worshipers experienced this same spiritual deadness, eventually leaving the fallout of global hunger, disease, and abuse of all kinds. What do you do with a dead plant that no longer bears fruit? What purpose does it serve, and what hope does it have? God would have been fair and just to dispose of Adam and Eve like dead plants into a compost pile, but his desire was not to discard humanity. Rather, it was to restore his people back to his presence. Though I could not restore the squash plant back to life in my garden, God had a plan to bring his people back into his presence. But this plan required perfection.

God would later give his people a set of rules to obey known as the Ten Commandments. But it was no use. They were deaf to the voice of God. Obedience is a fruit of being alive, and they were dead. They were incapable of obeying. These rules had no power to bring them back to life; they only made clear what was already known. They were spiritually dead. To think that obeying rules could have brought them back to life would be as if I looked my dead squash plant in the eyes and said, "You can live again as long as you produce again." It is true that if it produced again it would be alive, but the order is backward. It would first need to be made alive again to ever start producing.

The commandments may have had the appearance of a *quid pro quo* agreement, but that was only an illusion. If the plan for the law was to bring people back to life, then that plan was dead in the water before it ever had a chance (Galatians 3:21). If human fruitfulness is manifested by living within our design, and if being cut off from our life-source has prevented the possibility of fruit production, then how can producing more fruit graft us back into the root system? This is a logical fallacy. For us to have a chance at keeping the law, we would first need to be restored to the Father — our life-source. How could people reflect the image of God if their mirrors had been shattered beyond repair?

God was not giving the law to be a list of rules that, if kept, would magically bring them back to life. No, that would prove to be impossible. But maybe that was the point — to show everyone that trying to bring themselves back to life again was utterly impossible. Could my squash plant will itself back to life again by trying harder to produce squash? No. It would need to be grafted back into the root, and that's something it could never do on its own. Keeping the commandments has proven to be just as futile an effort in ancient days as it is today. While they do teach us where the boundary lines of God's design for humanity are, they give us no power to stay within those boundaries (Galatians 3:24, Romans 8:3)

Picture yourself standing on the summit of a mountain with nothing but snow and ice beneath your feet. There are no restraints or safety-harnesses; only a sign that reads, "Warning, sheer drop. Do not fall." Falling from this

32

distance would be certain death. To obey this sign most of the time would not be a viable option. There are no second chances here. It's either keep the rule all the time or bust. It's either life or death. Only a perfect record would keep you from falling off the mountain. Yet, there is a false idea that is popular in religion that if we keep the rules most of the time, we will be fine. But being mostly good isn't good enough. It only takes one offense to fall off the mountain. Just ask Adam and Eve. They fell from this holy mountain long ago. As descendants of Adam, we must not forget that the beginning of our journey starts at the bottom of the mountain, not at the top. How can we keep the rule of not falling off the mountain when we are at the bottom before we even start? Humanity is at the bottom with no hope of reaching the top. <u>Keeping the Ten Commandments is not only impossible for humans but also ineffective when it comes to restoring us to the Father.</u> What good is a set of rules that tells us not to fall off the mountain when we are already at the bottom? *Revealed the heart of mankind — " God knew David's heart. "*

Fruitless

Even though it's 2020, my family and I still like to listen to music on vinyl records and watch black and white classics. A few weeks ago, I walked into the family room and my daughter Marissa was watching an episode of "I Love Lucy." In this episode, Ricky and Lucy were more than an hour late for a dinner party they were invited to attend at the

Littlefield's house. Ricky and Lucy were mortified that they were so late, but more than that—they were famished.

Because they were so late, they missed out on the meal; but they didn't want it to be known how hungry they were. So, when the Littlefields stepped out of the room, Lucy, hoping to satisfy her hunger pangs, tried to sneak a bite of the fruit that was sitting in a fruit basket on the table. The problem, though, was that the fruit on the table was fake. It was plastic fruit that was made to look realistic. Mrs. Littlefield walked back into the room to find Lucy with a fake apple stuck to her teeth. Maybe the only thing worse than not having food in your belly, especially when you're hungry, is having your hopes set on food that turns out to be inedible.

Although humans were cut off from the life-source, that didn't stop them from trying to have the appearance of fruit anyway. Throughout history, humanity has been incapable of beholding God and becoming like him. They could not keep his law and bear real fruit apart from his life supply; so it was easier to fake it. God's fragmented people would do just this. They would manufacture fake fruit like pinning plastic squash to a dead plant. They went to the temple (the place where God and people could come together) to worship while simultaneously hoarding money from the widows and orphans who starved to death (Ezekiel 33). They would invoke the name of God, but their hearts were far from him (Isaiah 48). They would pray and fast while concurrently exploiting workers, arguing, and fighting with each other (Isaiah 58). They would tear their clothing to show how sorry they were for sinning, while their hearts were concocting their next sin (Joel 2). They would bring choice offerings to the temple, singing songs and playing instruments to God, while turning justice into bitterness and casting righteousness to the ground. God was not interested in this plastic, imitation fruit. In fact, he hated it.

"I hate, I despise your religious festivals; your assemblies are a stench to me. Even though you bring me burnt offerings and grain offerings, I will not accept them. Though you bring choice fellowship offerings, I will have no regard for them. Away with the noise of your songs! I will not listen to the music of your harps." – Amos 5:21-23 (NIV)

♫ He did not want to be worshipped in <u>pretense</u> but in <u>truth</u>. God did not want dead people to sing a song of praise as they pretended to be alive. God wanted them to be genuinely alive. He wanted his people to tear their hearts, not their clothes. The kind of fasting that God was interested in involved justice and benevolence, not just skipping a meal. The praise offering God desired was not found in a song, but in caring for the poor and needy. If they truly worshiped God, they would have been more concerned with loosening the chains of slaves, feeding the hungry, and clothing the naked; because true worship becomes what it beholds. God was angry at the sins of his people, but it is important to note the description of sins that angered God. He was not angered by their lack of religious piousness or activity but by their lack of justice and caring for their neighbor. True worship would manifest in the pursuit of mercy and justice for all because that's what is important to God. God's law made it clear that the problem with humanity was in the brokenness of their relationships.

Sin is always manifested through an abusive or broken relationship with God, with people, or with both. Sin is taking from others instead of giving to them. Murder is taking one's life, stealing is taking one's possessions, lust is taking one's dignity and purity, lying is taking one's truth, and committing each of these sins is taking worship away from God. These things completely contradict the image that we were designed to reflect. Yet, throughout history, God's people tried to conceal this brokenness with facades of religious rituals and traditions. And this misconception is still prevalent in religion today. Someone might attend church but curse his neighbor. Even a pastor or a priest might withhold from giving to the poor to sustain his lush lifestyle. This misunderstanding of spiritual fruitfulness can bolster a false security of having real fruit where there is none. God's law (and our purpose) is and always has been entirely focused on relationships. To put it simply, God's law for humanity is that we love. Yes, the entire law can be summarized in one phrase: "Love God and love people."

"'Love the Lord your God with all your heart and with all your soul and with all your mind. This is the first and greatest commandment. And the second is like it: 'Love your neighbor as

*yourself. **All the Law and the Prophets hang on these two commandments.**" – Matthew 22:37-40 (NIV)* ♌

This may sound like an oversimplification of the law, but on the contrary, it is emphatically stating the heart of the law's original intent—to love God and love people. This is the real fruit of living within God's proper design. This is the true image we were created to reflect. Since our purpose is to live fully within our design, and the laws of our design are summarized in these two commands, then we could settle this now. The chief purpose of man is to love God and love others. For it is in fulfilling this purpose that God is ultimately glorified, and humans are finally satisfied.

♌ *"Now all has been heard; here is the conclusion of the matter: Fear God and keep his commandments, for this is the duty of all mankind." – Ecclesiastes 12:13 (NIV)*

God doesn't want us to be religious; he wants us to be filled with love. He desires unity, peace, justice, and joy for all. But these things come from living within our design. They come only by living within our proper boundaries, not outside of them. Living within our design can only come from a heart that worships God. And this is the problem. Sin has separated us from him. We cannot truly know love if we don't know the Father (1 John 4:8). We can't stay within the boundaries of our design when we are miles away from it. We can't produce fruit when we are cut off from the root system. How can we reflect the image of God when the eyes of our worship have been blinded from seeing him for who he truly is?

This is why the Old Testament is filled with story after story of temples and tabernacles, kings and battles, bloodlines and sacrifices all for the purpose of restoring God's family to the way things were meant to be—in his presence, drinking from his fountain, worshiping at his feet, and reflecting the image that puts others before ourselves. Still today, we naturally do what Israel did throughout ancient history. We mask our fruitlessness with plastic images of fruit so that we can pacify God while feeling good about living our lives the way we want. We create a checklist of things that we think a Christian should do. We go to church, drop a handful of change in the Salvation Army bucket, read our devotionals, attend small groups, and assimilate to our Christian sub-cultures—hoping to receive God's tacit stamp of approval. We've found a way to cheat the system of pleasing God while pursuing our own kingdoms. We've found a way to sing our songs about God's love on the weekend, while our hearts are greedy for unjust gain; but God politely declines.

"My people come to you, as they usually do, and sit before you to hear your words, but they do not put them into practice. Their mouths speak of love, but their hearts are greedy for unjust gain. Indeed, to them you are nothing more than one who sings love songs with a beautiful voice and plays an instrument well, for they hear your words but do not put them into practice." – Ezekiel 33:31-32 (NIV)

Truth!!

For many years of my life, my ideas of what God wanted from me were misguided. I knew that God wanted me to come out of the world and "be holy as he is holy." I had been taught that I could avoid worldliness by abstaining from things like rated R movies, alcohol, tattoos, cussing, death metal, etc., I built fences to keep the devil's influence out of me without ever addressing the devil's influence that was already in the core of my bones. I was so concerned about keeping sin out that I neglected the fact that sin had already pervaded my entire soul. I was trying to protect my putrefied spirit from danger. I was trying to keep the world out of my heart, even though I was already a bona fide child of the world.

#1

So, what exactly constitutes sinfulness (or worldliness)? The heart of sinfulness is found neither in culture or victuals nor in the absence of religious platitudes or activities. The heart of sin is lust and pride (1 John 2:16). It is the result of a heart that does not worship God. It seeks selfish gain at the expense of someone else. It is the opposite of God's purpose for us—the opposite of loving God and loving people. Apart from God's life-source, we are all children of the world, regardless of how "clean-cut" or celibate we might be. If God is not the receiver of our worship, then we can only be defined by our worst sin. What hope do we have of bringing glory to God when we are utterly incapable of living within his design for our lives? What hope is there of ever producing real fruit when we are spiritually decomposing?

CHAPTER 3

THE WAY TO GOD

Discovering your purpose only to find that you are incapable of fulfilling that purpose is kind of like being given tickets to your favorite show for last night's admission. It brings a full spectrum of emotions that, unfortunately, leaves you on the wrong side of the spectrum. If we are on this earth to be image-bearing, fruit-producing beings, but we are unable to produce because we are passively decaying and spiritually festering, then what would be the point of trying? If there were no hope of fulfilling our God-given purpose, then we might as well pursue a self-destructive path of temporal pleasure. Why not pursue a life of happiness and joy elsewhere? For this reason—what brings joy to the dead but more death? What satisfies darkness but more darkness? For our totally depraved hearts, the pursuit of fulfillment leads only to a journey in the wrong direction. Happiness is never found in the pursuit of itself; it is a byproduct of fulfilling our true purpose (Psalm 16:11). Just as death desires the darkness and cringes at the light, so our broken worship desires only brokenness. But we were made to worship God. It is only by worshiping him that we are able to live within our true design and purpose. It is only through worshiping him that we can be totally fulfilled. But there is only one way to God — the way of perfection.

A Perfect Image

In the Vestfjord Valley, surrounded by towering mountains on every side, is the small Norwegian town of Rjukan. Between September and March every year, the mountains surrounding Rjukan completely block any direct sunlight from coming in, causing the town to be in the shadows of darkness for six months of the year. Residents had grown accustomed to living in the dark until a bookkeeper by the name of Oscar Kittilsen had the idea of installing giant mirrors on the mountainsides to reflect sunlight in the valley. By 2013, the sun-deprived town once again had access to the light of the sun. The mirrors brought hope and light where there was once only darkness.

Though sin shattered humanity like broken mirrors that once reflected the image of God, a new mirror had come to bring the hope of light to us once again. Though we were broken images of God, Jesus was the perfect image of the invisible God who broke through the heavens for us.

"The Son is the image of the invisible God, the firstborn over all creation." — Colossians 1:15 (NIV)

In Ezekiel 41-43, God gave Ezekiel a prophecy foretelling the coming of Jesus in all his perfection. God gave Ezekiel visions (two chapters' worth) of detailed descriptions and precise dimensions of a perfect temple, along with the regulations for all the sin and guilt sacrifices that would be made. Then Ezekiel saw a vision of God's glory and radiance, a visible image of the invisible God, filling the temple and all the land. He first saw God's requirement for perfection, then he saw someone fulfilling that requirement. Jesus would be the one to completely fulfill the requirement of God's perfect standard. In Ezekiel's vision, Jesus was the one sitting on his throne, living among his people, filling the temple; and there would be no shortcoming on his end. Where there was once a call for perfection, there would be a response of fulfillment. Ezekiel was told to share the comprehensive details of the temple to the sinful people of Israel so that the message of its perfection would cause them to be filled with shame and lead them to call on God for help.

If you've ever taken on any kind of project that was far beyond your ability, then you probably understand what was happening here. It would be like someone handing you the instructions for building the Taj Mahal and then telling you to get to work. Having the instructions alone is not nearly enough to complete this task. Exposing the comprehensive details of God's perfect temple would overwhelm the people of Israel into seeking his help. God gave us his law of perfection to expose our imperfection along with our need for rescue. But God didn't stop at sending the law. He also sent the one who would fulfill it.

If your church background is anything like mine, then you may have grown up thinking that the Bible was a collection of stories with morals to inspire you to overcome your giants and live right no matter what the cost. But the truth is that I am not the hero in any of the Bible stories. Jesus is. While we can learn from the faith that is modeled through these people in the Bible, the most important thing to see in each of them is Jesus. In each of these stories, I am the one in distress who needs to be rescued. In the story of David and Goliath, I'm not David. I'm probably more like one of David's brothers who were envious of him and laughed in his face. In the story of Daniel and the lion's den, I'm not Daniel. I would have buckled under pressure when I heard the words "Lion's den." The heroes in all the Bible stories are pointing us to the true hero—Jesus. The point of David's story is not that we would try to be more like David by defeating our giants; it's to point us to Jesus who would be the one to conquer the giant of death for us. The point of Daniel's story is not to teach us to be good like Daniel; it's to point us to Jesus—the one who would be wrongfully accused and thrown into the pit of the grave for three days. But the lion of death would have no power over Jesus because he would rise out of the pit. The same principle is true of Joseph, Noah, and every other hero in the Old Testament. You see, there is a hero—a chosen one—that the whole Bible is pointing towards, but it's not you or me. It's Jesus.

Jesus came to do what we could never do. He came to make us alive again and restore our purpose. He came to repair our broken worship and shape us back into the selfless image we were designed to be. God, the Maker of the universe, full of love and compassion for his creation, was unwilling that people should perish. Though we were already dead in our sins, the Author of life would stop at nothing to breathe new life into our lungs and make us fully alive once again. God had a plan. He sent Jesus.

The first time I met my wife, we were sitting across from each other at the dinner table of an Olive Garden restaurant. I was a senior in high school and my wife was a sophomore at the Bible college I would later attend. My wife is a first-degree extrovert, and I am exactly the opposite. She was sitting next to her friends at the table having a fun time, laughing, being herself; while I was quietly watching her, thinking to myself, "I'm going to marry this girl." By the time we left the restaurant, I'm fairly sure she still had no idea that I was even there. But I was smitten. She had every single quality that I found attractive. She was fun, playful, smart, always smiling, and just as beautiful inside as she was on the outside. I have never dated another girl since that day. I chose my wife because she possessed everything that I desired in a woman. And I was determined to marry her no matter what it took (which was a lot, by the way; but that story is for another day).

This is true of how people approach many things in life. We choose according to our standards. Whether choosing a future spouse or choosing who will be on our softball team, we have standards that inform who we will choose. I chose my wife because she blew my standard out of the water. You might choose someone to be on your softball team because that person is athletic and good at the sport. In a similar way, God had a standard that was acceptable for himself. That standard was perfection— complete flawlessness—nothing less would do. God looked for perfection in humanity and found none (Romans 3:10). So, he sent his own son, Jesus, to be the spotless lamb without any blemish. Jesus would be the new Adam that would start a new humanity. He would be the seed of a new people for himself because only Jesus met God's perfect standard. He would be the only man ever to live within the blueprint of God's intended design for humanity—the only human ever to walk the earth and fulfill the law (Matthew 5:17). God's law, which is summarized by "loving God and people," was fulfilled and fully embodied by none other than Jesus.

"He was chosen before the creation of the world, but was revealed in these last times for your sake." – 1 Peter 1:20 (NIV)

Price of Restoration

Jesus' perfect life is just as important to us as his death. In his death, he absorbed the sins of humanity; but in his resurrection, he brought the newness of life for all who would accept his terms. Maybe you're wondering why Jesus had to die in the first place, or why anyone had to die. If God was truly God, then why couldn't he just forgive and forget? Why would Jesus need to die for us at all?

The first reason Jesus had to die was to pay for our sin debt. Yes, Jesus forgave us, but forgiveness alone doesn't undo the damage that has been done. Forgiveness addresses the act that caused the damage, but it does not cover the damage itself. Forgiveness might excuse the behavior that shattered the mirror, but it does not repair the mirror.

A couple of years ago, my youngest son Colin was about eighteen months old. We had company over at our house, and we had all just finished eating dinner. The kids went into the next room to watch one of the Star Wars movies, while the adults conversed at the dinner table. A few moments later, something I saw out of the corner of my eye caught my attention. My son was holding a baseball bat that he had brought in the house from outside and was holding it over his head as if he were about to battle Darth Vader himself. Not once, but twice, Colin struck our 50" flat screen tv with the metal baseball bat. I jumped out of my seat to pull the bat out of his hand, but it was too late. A constellation of dead pixels now covered our less than six-month-old television. Though my son was oblivious to the damage he had caused, and though I was quick enough to forgive him for what he had done, none of this changed the fact that our tv was completely ruined. The damage was done. There was nothing either of us could say or do that would fix the tv.

Though we had broken God's laws and piled a mountain full of sin debt, he still sent his greatest and most treasured possession, Jesus, to absorb the wrath we deserved for stepping outside his design. He paid for the damage caused by the wrecking ball of sin with his own blood. Jesus lived the life we could never live and then suffered the death that we deserved on the cross. His words on the cross, "It is finished," ended the lifelong sin debt that humanity owed to God. Jesus covered the cost.

The second reason Jesus died was so he could be the seed of a new humanity. Jesus was born of a virgin, which meant he did not come from the same flawed seed as Adam. Jesus was the first-born of a new humanity. His was an untainted seed. Yes, he was fully man, but he was also fully God. He wasn't starting from the bottom of the mountain with a sinful nature; he started his journey from the top. Adam was the dead squash plant, but Jesus was the living vine. Jesus had to die, not just to pay for our sins, but also to be resurrected from the grave as the seed that was planted into the ground, to rise as the living vine that would be our new life source (John 12:24).

Humble Obedience

Jesus humbled himself to become obedient to death. Death had no authority over Jesus because he had never broken any of God's laws. He was God. Death had no power over him, yet he humbled himself to let death pull him under. This humility that he demonstrated was done out of his love for us. He died so we could live. Humility acted like the softening of a material, allowing himself to become weak and vulnerable enough to meet us where we are. He poured out his life to fill us with life. If Jesus had not humbled himself to die for us; we would have no hope. And it is in beholding the one who humbled himself to be obedient to death on our behalf that moves us to become humbly obedient in return.

"God opposes the proud but shows favor to the humble." — James 4:6 (NIV)

Jesus did not deviate from his godly character to humble himself; it was in his character to be humble. He did not step outside of his character to lay down his life; laying down his life was part of who he is. God did not hoard his most prized possession for himself; instead, he gave his only son to die on a cross to save his enemies. These things are important to remember when considering the fact that you become like what you worship. These are characteristics that would emanate from someone who worships Jesus.

Jesus humbled himself to be vulnerable as a way to invite us into his life. It requires humility and vulnerability from us to be joined together with him, just like a marriage where two people humble themselves to be joined together as one. As he humbled himself to die, we too must humble ourselves to die to our sins of pride and selfishness. It's as if Jesus stepped into the fire as a perfect mold and then invited us to step into the fire with him; so that we could be melted down and conformed into his image. As we examine his humility, it should lead us to humble ourselves and put our faith in him. Faith and humility work together in the process of being reborn. It's in the soil of humility that the seed of faith can flourish, and without faith, it is impossible to please God. Without faith, it is impossible to be made alive again to produce the fruit and bear the image for which we were designed.

If you were to fall into a ditch and were unable to climb out on your own, it would take humility to cry out for help and admit your need to be rescued. It would take faith to grab on to the rope that was dropped down by someone you couldn't see. It's only when we humble ourselves enough to call out to Jesus for help that we can begin to step into a life of faith in him as he pulls us out of the ditch.

Jesus calls out to us in our broken and lifeless condition and invites us to humbly bow to his power. We are like iron that must bow to the will of the blacksmith. We humbly rest our faith in his hands by submitting ourselves to his work in his way. He does the molding and the shaping; we do the submitting.

When my oldest son was a toddler, one of the things we would like to do together was to play with his "Little Tikes" basketball hoop. He loved having me as an audience to watch him perform, and we would both make the biggest deal of it every time he would make a shot. One of his favorite parts of playing basketball with me was dunking. He couldn't actually dunk it on his own, but he would ask me to pick him up and hold him so he could. I would put my hands under his arms and tell him to jump. Then, as I counted to three, he would jump as I carried his momentum up to the basket. He would do this a hundred times in a row if I let him, but it never came to that. I would be exhausted after five or six times because I was doing all the work. This is similar to the way it works with our faith, only God never gets tired. When we think about conforming to God's image, it might sound exhausting; but it doesn't need to be, because it's the Holy Spirit who does all the work. It's true that he commands us to obey, but once we take that leap of faith, he picks us up and carries us the rest of the way.

He wants us to rely on him — to jump at his command and let him carry us. He tells us to do crazy things like get baptized, give money to the poor, and help those who don't benefit us in return. He commands us to step into our purpose, but then, as we step, he is the one who does all the lifting. He commands us to pour out our love for other people as unto God, and as we demonstrate our obedience, it is the power of God in us that does the work. Jesus calls us to take up our cross and follow in his steps, but we can only take up our cross as we behold him on his.

"Then he said to them all: 'Whoever wants to be my disciple must deny themselves and take up their cross daily and follow me.'" — Luke 9:23 (NIV)

PART 2
PRODUCT OF WORSHIP

CHAPTER 4

A NEW CREATURE

According to Pew Research, Christianity is the largest religion in the world. It is estimated that more than 30% of the world's population (over two billion people) claim to have faith in Jesus. But in many cases, these verbal professions of faith are the only evidence of that faith. 2 Corinthians 5:17 teaches that if anyone is in Christ, that person is a new creation. Becoming a new creature implies that it is something different than it was before. In Christ, we are no longer old creatures. We are new. But if faith in Christ does not come with new behaviors, then this kind of faith is as inconsequential as believing in Santa Clause or Big Foot. It is easy to hear the story of Jesus and respond with the words "I believe," as we continue living our lives exactly as they were. But here is the problem. Churches have become filled with people who claim to worship Jesus in the same way that a nominal sports fan who never watches a single game claims to be a die-hard enthusiast. These words are empty. Jesus said, "All who call on the name of the Lord will be saved;" so we send up a prayer like we were signing a contract that would be stored away in a forgotten filing cabinet somewhere. But this is not true worship. This is not what genuine faith in Jesus looks like. So then, what does this new creation look like? How can you spot it? How can you become it?

Hidden in Him

As Jesus was hanging with his arms spread open on a cross, he became a lightning rod of God's wrath. Like an eagle spreading his wings over the nest to protect his eaglets, Jesus spread open his wings to protect us as he absorbed the fiery arrows of God's wrath that were being poured out over our sin. The only protection from the arrows is found directly beneath the cross, under his wings. Only those under his wings will be protected. From God's perspective, all who are hidden in Jesus are considered one with Jesus. His perfection covers our imperfections.

"He will cover you with his feathers, and under his wings you will find refuge;" – Psalm 91:4 (NIV)

Being hidden in Christ is our only hope both for escaping the deadly arrows of God's wrath and being resurrected into a life that produces lasting fruit. Being hidden in Christ, found in Christ, a follower of Christ — however you want to put it — can be a confusing thing to grasp; not because it is inherently difficult to understand, but because it has been nuanced to the point of confusion.

What does it really mean to be hidden in Christ? What does genuine faith look like? Let me illustrate this with a story.

There were three groups of people who lived on an island. It was a beautiful, tropical paradise rich in natural resources with everything you could ever want or need. People rarely came or left the island before now. But, sadly, the island was diseased. It was sinking every day by the foot, and it was only a matter of time before the island and everything on it would be completely decimated. But there was hope. A rescue vessel came to the island to bring salvation. The captain of the ship knew the island was sinking and would eventually swallow every person whole. He came to bring hope and rescue to all.

As each group of people saw the rescue ship in the harbor, here is how they responded:

The first group heard the news of the rescue ship's arrival but chose not to leave. They knew the island might sink, but the riches of the island and all they had spent their lives working for was too much to throw away and abandon. They counted the cost and decided that they loved the island too much to let her go. Ignorance was bliss. So, group one continued to go about their lives on the sinking island. They weren't going anywhere.

The second group had seen first-hand the condition of the island. Sure, they loved the island, too, and all the possessions they had accumulated; but they would rather be poor and alive than be rich and dead. Plus, rumor had it that the island to which this rescue boat would return was every bit as heavenly as their island; maybe even more heavenly.

So, group two gladly left all their wealth of toys and pleasantries behind as they ran to the safety of the ship without even looking back.

The third group was the largest group by far. They knew the island was sinking, and they had every intention of getting on the ship. But this group of people didn't respond with quite the same urgency as the previous group. Although they evacuated their homes in the center of the island, they did not get in the boat. Instead, they set up camp on the beach next to the harbor where the rescue boat was. Though they set up camp right next to the boat, they didn't get in the boat. They built campfires on the beach and held their parties while clapping hands and singing songs about being rescued from the sinking island. Some of them would start to doubt their security and feel anxious, but the others in the group would console them with reminders that the rescue ship was right in front of them and that they had no reason to worry. However, the island would eventually sink, and only those who were on the boat would be rescued. Not even those in group three would survive.

In this parable-like tale of the sinking island, Jesus is the heroic captain of the rescue ship, sent from his Father to seek and to save that which was lost. Group one is the group of people who have chosen to decline a lifestyle that includes God or his rules. This group does not necessarily consist of people who would say that they hate God, but rather people who worship creation instead of the Creator. They genuinely desire the things of this world and are not willing to leave it behind, like a moth who can't resist the splendor of the light.

This group will sadly die before they ever have a chance to live.

The true followers of Christ are in group two. They were not rescued because of any work they contributed to the rescue mission. They were rescued because they put their complete trust in the rescue boat, not just in theory but also in action. They left all they had behind and hid in the safety of their rescuer. If the story were to continue, the people of group two would also take on the rescuing qualities of their captain, combing the coastline from the rescue ship, searching for those in need of rescue.

Group three, the largest group, has tried to find a compromise of being rescued from this fallen world while simultaneously enjoying its treasures. But this romanticized way of thinking brings only a false sense of rescue and nothing more. Group three is made up of people who might have said a prayer to ask Jesus in their heart, even though their actions deny God. This group is filled with people who have given into an "American Dream" brand of Christianity that is pervasively accepted. They have a false security of salvation because they have checked off the boxes on a list of things that their manufactured version of God wants them to do. But here's the thing—being hidden in Christ is not about how much faith you have or how much you've done; it is about who you are trusting with your life. It is about who you choose to worship. It's about where you stand—either in the boat or on the island. The third group is neither fully committed to getting on the boat nor fully committed to staying on the island. But their fate will be the same as those in the first group. They just haven't realized it yet.

> *"So, because you are lukewarm – neither hot nor cold – I am about to spit you out of my mouth. You say, 'I am rich; I have acquired wealth and do not need a thing.' But you do not realize that you are wretched, pitiful, poor, blind and naked." – Revelation 3:16-17 (NIV)*

I do want to give one caveat. Some people may not fully identify with either group two or group three. To those who struggle with sin and fight to keep the faith, let me say, that struggling is a good sign of being in group two and not in group three. Group three does not struggle to fight sin; their only struggle is to conceal their sin while they continue walking in it. Though we all sin, not all people choose to struggle and fight with it. Fighting against sin is evidence of the Holy Spirit's presence. If there were no fight, then there would be no victory. My hope is not to cause you to doubt the authenticity of your faith, but to challenge you to go deeper into it – to trust God wholeheartedly, not just with words and songs, but with everything.

Being hidden in Christ is more than a mantra you sing about on Sunday mornings or a label you identify with during a discussion that may come up at the office. Being hidden in Christ is a complete identity transformation from one image into another. Once we were sinking, but now we are rescued. Once we were on the island, but now we are on the boat. Once we were dead in our sins but now made alive in Christ.

"Since, then, you have been raised with Christ, set your hearts on things above, where Christ is, seated at the right hand of God. Set your minds on things above, not on earthly things. For you died, and your life is now hidden with Christ in God." — *Colossians 3:1-3 (NIV)*

To be hidden *in* something (or with something) is to be in agreement with it. It suggests a conforming to that thing — like being in a car.

When you are in a car, you are, in a way, at one with the car. Where the car goes, you go. If the car goes fast you go fast, and if it turns left, you turn left with it. It would be impossible to turn right when the car is turning left unless you were not actually *in* the car. Being *in* Christ is this way. Only, it is important to remember that we are not in the driver's seat. He is. So then, making the turns with the car (Jesus) is more about surrender and submission than it is about driving. To be in something is to say that you are in subjection to that thing. That thing is driving the car. It is sitting on the throne of your heart. You've given that thing or person the authority to call the shots in your life, and you are giving yourself over to be mastered by it. To be hidden in Christ is to worship Christ; because to be hidden in him means that what is true of him becomes true of us.

Jesus came to restore our broken worship and make us whole, giving us yet another reason to worship him. He was the only perfect image and the only way back to God, and he laid down his perfect record in exchange for our death sentence. When we were left for dead, he came to us like a good Samaritan, giving up his own life to resuscitate ours. He pulled the car over and offered us a ride back to God in the passenger seat. It is only when we are hidden in and in step with him that we can be restored to the Father. It's about submission. It's saying, "I'm willing to ride on your merit and not my own." So, Jesus says, "Let's go. Follow me. Do as I do. Fix your eyes on me and become like me."

Just like the saying, "You are what you eat," we become what we worship. It is the same basic concept, only on a grander scale. When we are captured by the vision of Jesus and what he did for us through his death on the cross, we are given a call to worship him. It's a call to repent from sin and live in the light of freedom. The choice to worship Jesus is a choice to repent from our sin. We don't repent to earn God's favor; we repent to receive the favor we have already been offered.

Repentance is not simply a feeling of remorse; it is the redirecting of our worship. It is a change of mind that materializes through a change of action (James 2:18). To repent means that we turn away from idols and fix our gaze on the love of Jesus. It means we turn away from the sins of pride and selfishness and turn to a life of humility and selflessness. We turn away from greed and turn to generosity. We turn from anger and turn to kindness and patience. We turn from callousness and turn to compassion.

We do these things as a response to beholding his love for us. The more we behold his love for us, the more we will desire to walk in his love. God does not only desire that we walk in love, but that we walk in love from the heart.

"Now that you have purified yourselves by obeying the truth so that you have sincere love for each other, love one another deeply, from the heart. For you have been born again, not of perishable seed, but of imperishable, through the living and enduring word of God." – 1 Peter 1:22-23 (NIV)

True Worship

The Father said he was looking for true worshippers who worship in spirit and truth. He is not looking for fake ones but real ones. God desires authentic worship. A true worshipper is one who is filled with thankfulness, hidden in the shadow of Jesus' wings. A true worshipper willfully conforms to the mold of God's image, both in spirit and in truth.

"God is spirit, and his worshipers must worship in the Spirit and in truth." – John 4:24 (NIV)

Let me break this down.

God is a spirit; so, we must come to him in spirit. We must worship by the power of the Holy Spirit and with a spirit of sincere desire and passion. We must not forget that ever since the Garden of Eden, the spirit of man has been cut off from the Father. We would need a new breath of life breathed into the hollowness of our spirit (John 3:5). And it's through our response of humble submission to Jesus' love that the Spirit of God brings us back to life. He removes our heart of stone and replaces it with a heart of flesh (Ezekiel 36:26). He removes our dead spirit and replaces it with his living Spirit.

The Holy Spirit ignites a fire within us, causing our hearts to desire him above everything else. He opens our blind eyes and awakens true worship within us that is full of passion and desire to obey him. God doesn't want plastic versions of our worship; he wants the real thing. He doesn't desire external sacrifices and offerings; he desires a broken and contrite heart (Psalm 51:17). God doesn't want your hands until he has your heart. He is not impressed by consistent church attendance, CCM radio presets, or the amount of money you put in the offering plate. God wants your undying devotion and desire. After he has your heart, these things might be pleasant to him but not before.

"These people honor me with their lips, but their hearts are far from me." – Matthew 15:8 (NIV)

To worship him in spirit means that we worship him through the power of the Holy Spirit with all of our inner-being. When we repent of our sins, the Holy Spirit moves in, and the dead spirit of our father Adam moves out. The Holy Spirit becomes our spirit, and he awakens our heart's desire to worship the Father.

A true worshipper also worships in truth. There are a couple of different ways to interpret or apply "truth" from this verse, and I think they are both correct and work together.

The first and most obvious *truth* is Jesus himself. Jesus said, "I am the way, the TRUTH, and the life." Jesus is the truth; so, all who come to the Father must come through him—his blood, his work, and his authority (John 14:6). He is the only exit from sin's prison cell and the only entrance into the kingdom of God. Jesus is the ark that rides the flood of God's wrath. We must be in him to come to the Father. So, to worship the Father, we must worship in truth, which is to say, we must worship *in* Jesus. We must be hidden in him. Jesus is our passage to eternal life. He is the truth and the ultimate authority. Whatever he says to be true is true. Jesus has established and preserved the Scriptures to be this authority for us. So, to worship in truth, we must worship Jesus by the wisdom of his Word.

The second understanding of "truth" would be to say, "in actuality." It's the physical manifestation of worship—the "becoming." In other words, it is putting your money where your mouth is—the marriage of belief and action—the agreement of the physical with the spiritual. If I were to say that I believed one thing but acted in a way that was inconsistent with that belief, I would either be considered a hypocrite or a fool. If a belief does not inform the way I live, then it is not a genuine belief. Although some beliefs may have little to no consequence or future implication to the way we live our life, belief in Jesus is not this way. If worship is valuing one thing above everything else, then true worship in Jesus would mean that we give him our thoughts, attention, desires, and obedience. Saying we worship Jesus without actually worshiping him is not true worship. That would be like saying we were in the boat when in reality we were still on the beach.

What, then, does the physical action of true worship look like? In many churches, *worship* is described as a Sunday gathering or an act of singing. But based on the explanation above, even singing isn't true worship unless it is first coming out of a spirit of authenticity. True worship is responding to what God has done for us in the way that he has prescribed. The physical response of worship to the revelation of Jesus is to mirror him. It is to fix our gaze and affection on him and allow the essence of his person to transform us. It is to obey his truth with humble submission by becoming more like him. One that worships in spirit and truth is one who worships with a whole heart by the power of the Holy Spirit through obedience to Jesus' commands that are found in his Word. A true worshipper is one who, being hidden in Christ, gladly and willfully conforms to his image. It is cause and effect. We behold, and we become.

In John 21, after Jesus' resurrection, he appeared to his disciples several times. The third time he appeared to them, after they had just finished eating a meal together, Jesus said to his disciple Simon Peter, "Simon, do you love me?" Simon replied, "Yes, Lord, you know that I love you." Jesus said, "Feed my lambs." Then Jesus repeated the same question again, "Simon, do you love me?" Simon must have been slightly confused, but he replied, "Yes, Lord, you know I love you." Jesus said, "Then take care of my sheep." A third time, Jesus asked Simon, "Do you love me?" Simon Peter was hurt that Jesus would ask him the same question a third time. Though Jesus undoubtedly was giving Simon a chance to redeem himself after having denied Jesus three times at the cross, there was something else happening here.

Jesus told his disciple Peter that if he genuinely loved him, he would feed his sheep. In other words, if Peter loved Jesus, Peter would do the very thing that Jesus did. He would become passionate about the same things that Jesus was passionate about. If Peter loved Jesus, he would care for the people Jesus cared for. He would make necessary sacrifices to love and watch over those who identified with Jesus. A love for Jesus is not passive. It actively reciprocates. This is consistent with what Jesus told Phillip in John 14:15. He told Phillip that the way to show love to God is by loving his neighbor. The beholding of Christ's love ultimately leads to becoming a reciprocator of that love towards our neighbor. True worship is an expression of love because it is produced by love. As we see the way Jesus laid down his life for us, we, too, can lay down our lives in response. Jesus demonstrated his love for us by taking up his cross, and we take up our cross to follow Jesus by demonstrating his love towards others.

Though true worship may produce loud singing in church with hands lifted in surrender to God, we must not miss that the worship Jesus desires is expressed through loving our neighbor from the heart. In my years of vocational worship ministry, I've seen what it looks like to love the idea of worship without really worshiping. There are those who worship a form of worship itself. They love the music and the experience—the raw emotion and the energy. They love to go wild during a worship service, but after the service, they go to a restaurant and yell at their waiter for messing up their order. Don't get me wrong. I love and value music as much as anybody—maybe more. But as a worship pastor, I would be doing a disservice to cheapen the true worship that God desires. Jesus didn't say, "If you love me, sing loudly." He said, "If you love me, take care of my sheep." If we love Jesus—if we truly worship him—we will love. Passion for a worship experience is not a substitute for true worship.

True worship happens as a response to the revelation of God's goodness by turning away from what kills us and running towards what saves us. It turns from pride and runs to humility. It turns from selfishness and runs towards selflessness. Worship has no off switch. Either we are worshiping Jesus or something else. And it's in the turning to Jesus, both in spirit and in truth, that God's living water breaks through heaven's flood gates and pours into our souls. It's in turning to Jesus where true worship begins. This is where eternal life starts. This is where freedom is found (2 Corinthians 3:17). This is the beginning of fulfilling your purpose. Stepping into the waters of baptism is the beginning of stepping into his mold. This journey may start with a simple prayer, but it doesn't end there. It always leads to true worship.

A New Identity

In 1946, a young couple by the name of Paul and Clara were married shortly after his return home from serving in the Coast Guard during World War II. Paul was a blue-collar mechanic who always had a garage full of cars. He loved tinkering and figuring out new things. His wife Clara was a bookkeeper. The two of them didn't have much money, but they loved each other. Their love for each other overflowed into a desire to grow their family, but after an ectopic pregnancy, it seemed that adoption would be their best option. So, in 1955, Paul and Clara adopted a little boy.

This little boy captured the hearts of his mom and dad, and their love for him captured his heart as well. He grew up watching his dad constantly working on cars and building things. If his mom ever wanted something fixed in the house, he'd watch his dad fix it. If she wanted something built, he'd watch as his dad designed and build it. He loved hanging out and spending time with his dad; so, his dad sectioned off part of the garage to be a workshop just for him. This became a place for him to tinker while gleaning inspiration and creativity from his dad. This little boy would eventually grow to be one of the most creative and influential game-changers in all the world of technology. His name was Steve Jobs.

In the eyes of young Steve Jobs, there was no greater hero than his father. He admired his father and wanted his approval more than anything else. He studied his creative process and ingenuity to the point of becoming just like him. This revelation and admiration lead to his transformation.

"Therefore, be imitators of God, as beloved children." – *Ephesians 5:1 (ESV)*

When we were hopeless orphans in our sin, God loved us so much that he paid the ultimate price to adopt us as his own. He desired to bring us into his family and share all of his riches with us. He longs for us to be in his presence and be showered with his goodness and love. He wants what is unequivocally best for us, just as most parents would desire for their own. This has been his desire since the beginning of time. And with the wisdom and knowledge of the whole universe, he not only desires what's best for us, but he also knows exactly how to give it to us.

When we break his rules, he doesn't threaten to throw us out on the street. God's wrath-induced anger was completed at the cross. His only anger comes now when we refuse to receive his blessing and act as though we don't belong to him. His anger at our sin is rooted in his love for us. His love is not based on our performance; it is based on his character. He doesn't love us because we have earned it. He loves us because he is love. When God redeemed us back into his family, he gave us more than just a new last name (Isaiah 43:1). He gave us a new identity, new desires, and a new purpose. He gave us a new image.

Children who have been raised by small business owners know all too well that whether or not you are an official employee, being part of the family makes you part of the family business. As a pastor's kid, I was always at church. And now as a church staff member myself, my children are growing up being among the first to arrive at church and the last to leave every week. We plan our vacations around the church calendar. This is all just a way of life for us. My children love music; some of them play instruments. Family worship time and singing together are as common as playing outside for us. We do these things because it's who we are.

When we were adopted into the family of God, we were brought into what the family does. We conform to the family business like a branch that was grafted into a vine. We take on the identity, the work, and the undeniable aroma of belonging to him. Being in Christ means we are part of his family. And being in God's family brings a whole new identity. Being in his family shapes everything about us. God's purpose to bring reconciliation becomes our purpose. His passion to love and care for people becomes our passion. His work of bringing justice where there is none becomes our work.

I've heard people say that they are okay with the God of the New Testament but not the God of the Old Testament. They are okay with the Jesus who eats meals with sinners and heals sick people, but not the God who buried the earth's population in the great flood and unleashed armies to wipe out entire cities. Though it may seem at times like God was bipolar or just downright mean in the Old Testament, there has never been a time in all of history when God didn't love people and abhor their sin. He has always been passionate about his own glory and for pure justice wherever injustice might be found. The books of prophets may appear to be full of doom and gloom with chapter after chapter of warnings of destruction, but let's not miss the long-suffering that was shown through the hundreds of years of God's warning people to turn back to him.

"For his anger is but for a moment, and his favor is for a lifetime..." – Psalm 30:5 (ESV) ♡

Yes, God was angry at their sin, but he was slow to be angry. His patience was more. God doesn't desire that any should die, but that all would turn back to him (2 Peter 3:9). He is full of compassion, love, and forgiveness. God's business since the beginning of time was to gather a family together who would worship him in his presence within the boundaries of his design. Every chapter of the Bible points to this end—a new heaven and earth where harmony is restored to the way it was in the Garden of Eden. This is what God is doing, and this is what his children do.

Being a child of God has more implications than just reaping the benefits of being in his family. It transforms the way we see and treat everyone around us. What's important to him becomes important to us. He adopts the orphan, tends to the widow, listens to the child, heals the leper, feeds the hungry, and cares for the poor and needy. This is who he is, and this is who we become. In Christ, our money becomes a tool, not an idol. Our influence becomes a force of change, not a spotlight of fame. Our homes become a beacon for the hurting, not a buffer from it.

We were prisoners until God set us free. We were outcasts until he wrapped his robe around our shoulders. We were poor and needy until he prepared a place for us at his table with princes (Psalm 113). Now we have been brought into the family who continues to do these things for others. The God who loves us transforms us to be a people who love others. The God who adopted us when we were orphans without a home leads us to adopt orphans into our own homes. The God who demonstrated selflessness and gentleness leads us to this same kind of selflessness and gentleness to those around us. The God who forgave us in our wrongdoings leads us to forgive others for doing wrong to us.

In Colossians 3, Paul contrasts a picture of the old self with the new self. He compares our old, orphan garments to our new, adopted garments. He said to take off the old and put on the new. Jesus pulled us out of the gutter and gave us a seat at his table. He handed us clean clothes to replace our old, tattered rags. The old garments were stained with sexual immorality, impurity, lust, and evil desires; and wreaked of greed, anger, rage, slander, and idolatry. We are to put on the new garments of mercy, kindness, humility, gentleness, and patience. And above all, we are to clothe ourselves with love; because love is the fabric that holds all the other new garments together (Colossians 3:14). As we behold Jesus and fix our eyes on him, we become more like him.

"Do not lie to each other, since you have taken off your old self with its practices and have put on the new self, which is being renewed in knowledge in the image of its Creator." – Colossians 3:9-10 (NIV)

In the book of John, Jesus was called the light of the world. He came to be a light in the darkness exposing our brokenness and opening our eyes to his healing. And just as a light that enters a room lights up the faces of everyone in the room, Jesus projected his light onto our faces so that we could become conductors of light for others. We are like glow in the dark objects that absorb energy from his light source. He lights up our faces with the light of his love so that his light emanates from us everywhere we go, creating a chain reaction. When the light comes in, the light will shine out. When we are hidden in Christ, his spirit glows out of us. When we are filled with his love, his love will flow from us, touching those around us. It's not just something we do; it's who we are. We are children of light.

You will see this same kind of transformational worship when you look at an overzealous sports fan. When a fan becomes consumed by his favorite team, he watches all the games. The team eventually takes over the fan's thoughts, conversations, bumper stickers, wardrobes, and coffee mugs. The fan pours his money into season tickets and gives increasingly of his time digging into news stories and articles related to this team. He can't get enough of them. It becomes his identity. This is the way we are all designed. Our identity defines what we do. What we think about is what will fuel our heart's desires and command our actions. What goes in eventually comes out.

Think of a cup. If you were to fill a cup to the brim with water and continue pouring, the water would begin to spill over the edges and touch everything around it. When you fill yourself with something, that thing will eventually take over and overflow until it touches those around you.

When the water we are drinking from is the living water of Jesus, it not only fills us with life, but it also transforms our thoughts, conversations, passions, and actions. When our worship is pointed to him, we are able to snap into the grooves of our intended design. We adapt to the Creator's blueprint and begin to live within our true purpose. This is what we were made for. It doesn't require a master's degree or a theological masterclass to live within our design. It takes drinking in from the love of God through the revelation of Jesus to begin fulfilling our purpose as humans.

I was raised in a family where chivalry was not dead. My father taught my two brothers and me to open doors for ladies and the elderly as a sign of respect. We never hit girls, and we always walked on the outside of the sidewalk so that if a car drove by, the boys would become a mud-shield for the girls. To this day, my wife still waits in the car until I come around to open her door for her. Not because she's a prima-donna, but because she knows I want to show her honor and respect. This is baked into who I am, and I plan to raise my boys the same way. My boys don't really have a choice in the matter. Being an Azzarello boy means treating all ladies and elderly people with this kind of respect and honor. It's who we are.

Being a member of God's family means going against the grain of what our old, orphan-nature might tell us. We may be tempted to protect our emotions by saving our love for the people we know most, but the gospel teaches us to give it away to all people in all situations. When our identity is found in Christ, we don't need to know someone deeply to show them love; we need only to know the love of the Father. The love that led him to lay down his Son for his enemies is the same love we are called to walk in. It's the same love that fills us. And only out of beholding his love for us are we able to know what true love is.

The Father showed his love for us, not only to save us from our brokenness but also to adopt us back to the family that we were made for; thus, restoring our purpose to love him in return. And the way we love the Father is by showing his love to those around us; not only to our close friends and family but also to our enemies and those who offer nothing in return.

Our orphaned condition taught us to only love those who can benefit us, but our new identity in God's family tells us that every single person no matter what age, race, or gender is worthy of our undying love; because this is what our new family does. Although it is not in showing our love to people that makes us part of God's family or even secures our keep in his family, it is the fruit that comes as a result of being in the family. It's not what we do that defines who we are, but it is who we belong to that defines what we do.

CHAPTER 5

A NEW PURPOSE

Every year, thousands of high school graduates are faced with the daunting task of deciding their career paths, setting the trajectory of their work careers for the rest of their lives. From the college they attend to the field of study in which they enroll, these young adults solidify their decisions with student loans that they will often still be paying off for decades to come. These students are pursuing paths that either cater to their passions or serve as a means to accommodate their passions.

Some might choose to enter the medical field because they want to help people, or they might choose that field because they believe it will pay the bills in a meaningful way while simultaneously accommodating their desired lifestyle. Others may choose one of the arts because it's interesting or fun. Regardless of why they choose their path, the quest to discover their purpose or fulfill their calling in this life is one that probably resonates with most (if not all) of us. Even as young children, this quest begins with statements like, "When I grow up, I want to be a..." Though our passions and desires may change with age, the insatiable pursuit of fulfilling our purpose never does. It is something that is baked into all of us.

Though we all have a different calling on a micro-level, there is a common purpose that we all share on the macro. How do we measure or discern our calling? Before we can do this, we must be able to define what a successful life is. If living a successful life is in fulfilling our purpose, then finding our calling is the pathway we take to get there. There is a direct correlation between living a successful life and living out our calling, but to find our calling we first must understand what it means to live a successful life.

We naturally tend to define success (even if only implicitly) by standards of affluence, happiness, or renown. We measure it by the amount of money in our bank account or the number of subscribers on our YouTube channel. Malcolm Forbes, a famous American entrepreneur and millionaire, coined his own definition of success with this popular quote, "He who dies with the most toys wins." While Forbes certainly would have been a contender for the person with the most toys, he would still have to leave his toys behind as he bowed to the power of death at age 70. You could say that he found his calling but missed his purpose. As Thomas Merton said, "People may spend their whole lives climbing the ladder of success only to find, once they reach the top, that the ladder is leaning against the wrong wall."

Maybe your standard of success is a little more modest. Living a long, happy, and healthy life might be what success looks like in your book; therefore, your calling would be any vehicle that gets you there. But there is a problem with writing our own definitions of success for our lives. And that is—it's already been written. Trying to rewrite or rewire the purpose of humanity is like planting an apple tree and hoping for it to grow watermelons.

We were wired to serve a specific purpose, and regardless of what we may want that purpose to be, we cannot rewrite the definition of what it means to be fully human because we don't hold the pen. Only the Author of humanity can define its success. And he defines it as loving the Lord with all our being and loving our neighbor as ourselves. Therefore, we can say that we all have the same purpose as each other. While we don't all have the same calling, we do all have the same purpose. Our purpose is to worship God and bear his image. Our purpose is to conform to the mold that loves God and people.

Though everyone has the same purpose from a thirty-thousand-foot view, we were all uniquely gifted to live out a calling that looks different for each person. One might be gifted to be generous and another to be a teacher. The generous person finds her calling in recognizing the needs of people and helping to meet those needs; while the teacher uses his gifts to teach others to walk in love by using their own giftings. Either way, we all have the purpose of loving God and loving people, but one is called to show love through being generous while the other shows love through teaching. This is not to say that we aren't all to be generous or teach to some degree, but on a greater scale of "calling,"

If you knew God would immediately grant your prayer . . . ?

we each have an individual focus that is more pointed in a specific direction. Understanding your purpose (to love) is paramount. Once you understand your purpose, then your gifts and passions can help lead you to find your specific calling.

Let's dive a little deeper into understanding our purpose.

Love God

When the religious people asked Jesus which of the commands was the greatest of all, he responded, "Love the Lord your God with all your heart, soul, and strength." The idea that God would command our love challenges our modern, Disney-influenced way of thinking about the very word. If love is reduced to a fleeting emotion brought on by physical attraction, then it would not be something we could manufacture at will. But true love goes beyond superficial attraction or serotonin levels. True love happens when our heart, soul, and strength are in harmony with God. Let me break that down.

First, we are to love God with all our hearts. Remember, the heart of man is the fountain from which everything flows. If we are to love God at all, it must first begin in our hearts. The heart is where our passions and desires are formed, and it is at the helm of our worship. For the love of God to capture our hearts, our hearts need to be exposed to the undying love of God for us. Just like any relationship, time spent with someone produces more knowledge of that person. And this knowledge, whether good or bad, will influence your emotions towards that person. If you spent a day with someone who annoyed you, there is a chance that after spending a month with that person your annoyance will have multiplied. However, if your time is spent with the one who embodies the purest form of good and the source of all life, then the depth of your knowledge will inevitably heighten the roof of your affection towards that person.

I know my wife more deeply than I did when we first started dating. Over time we have shared experiences together that have led to increased knowledge of her beauty that I didn't have at the start of our relationship. Hence, my love for her now far outweighs the love I had for her back then. Our hearts are responders, not initiators. The more knowledge about someone that is exposed to our hearts, the more deeply our hearts can respond with affection. If we are to love God with our hearts, we must spend time with him and allow our hearts to be exposed to a deeper knowledge of who he is.

Second, we are to love God with our souls. This means that we love God with our entire being. We are mind, body, and spirit; and the sum of these things equals our soul. We are not only to love God with our hearts but also with our thoughts, words, bodies, and actions. Loving God with our soul means that we love God with every second of every minute of every day. In our work, in our rest, and in our play, we are to love the Lord. This does not mean that every

Spending time w/ Someone

thought and every word must include the word "Jesus," but it does mean we never forget that he is our first love.

Let me illustrate.

I am happily married to my wife of fifteen years. There are many times when I am at work or the store when I am not actively in a conversation with my wife. She may not even be in the middle of my every thought, but that does not mean that I forget we are married to each other when I pass by another woman. It is the commitment of love to my wife that keeps me from entertaining the thought of pursuing another woman in a romantic way. This doesn't mean the temptation never comes; it just means that when the temptation does come, I do not act on it.

In the same way, when Jesus is our first love, we will not forget it when an idol tries to seduce us. We may have a moment of temptation that challenges our faithfulness, and at times we will inevitably be unfaithful to God. But these moments lead us to remember that God has never been unfaithful to us. God foresaw that we would be unfaithful, but his love for us is always willing to forgive us and take us back (Hosea 2). He saw our unfaithfulness from the cross, and still, he hung in our place. This love is what drives us back to him. It's what arrests the gaze of our worship. And when he has the love of our soul, we will live our entire life—mind, body, and spirit—in the reality of our commitment to him.

Lastly, we are to love the Lord with our strength. This means that we are to love him with everything we have that is beyond who we are. It means that we love him with our stuff. In other words, we love him with our money, our networks, our influence, our vehicles, and our houses. We love God first with our hearts, then with our souls, and then with all of the resources at our disposal. This is consistent with the way we think about worship. Worship first begins in the heart, then it moves to our voices and actions, and lastly, it takes over our time, resources, and influence.

In the story, "The Count of Monte Cristo," Edmond Dantes washes up on shore after having escaped prison on the Island of Château d'If, only to enter the presence of aggravated pirates who were preparing to execute a traitor by the name of Jacopo. The crew was fond of Jacopo, but the captain could not allow his disloyalty to go unpunished. Edmond Dantes appeared to the captain like a ram in the bush who could receive the punishment in place of Jacopo. The captain forced Dantes and Jacopo into a knife duel, knowing that Jacopo was the greatest knife-fighter around. However, in an unexpected turn of events, Dantes pinned Jacopo and plunged his knife into the sand next to him. Though the fight was supposed to end with only one survivor, Dantes spared Jacopo's life. Jacopo realized the gift of mercy that he had been given, and in light of this revelation, offered his eternal indebtedness as a servant to Dantes. Jacopo was faced with a death sentence that resulted in his freedom. This gratitude materialized into his desire to serve Dantes with his whole life. The vision of what he had been given created an overwhelming thankfulness in his heart that led to a lifelong commitment to Dantes.

Loving God with all our heart, soul, and strength is the essence of true worship. It begins with beholding God's mercy toward us that leads to an undying affection and passion for serving him. The important word in the imperative, "love the Lord with all your heart, soul, and strength," is the adjective "all." This does not mean that we cannot love other things also, it simply means that the love of God informs and permeates the way we love everything else.

How does the 10 Comm. Speak into Worship.

God's first command in the <u>Ten Commandments</u> is that we must have no other gods before him. To elevate and love any one thing above God is an egregious violation of this command. It has been said that in breaking any one of the commandments, the first one would also be broken every single time. For anything to take over the throne of our hearts besides God would be idolatry. That spot is reserved for God and no one else.

When we remember our commitment to God with the things that he has given us, and when we honor his boundaries for our design, we show our love and dedication to him. For example, before eating a delicious meal, we can show our love to him simply by giving him thanks for his provision and by honoring his boundary to stop eating when we are full. By honoring his design for us, we can show our love in every aspect of life.

"So whether you eat or drink or whatever you do, do it all for the glory of God." — 1 Corinthians 10:31 (NIV)

81

(margin handwritten note: BOOM)

God created good things to point us to his goodness. He gives us good things so we can enjoy him through those things. He never intended for us to enjoy his gifts (i.e., food, drink, work, play, sex, music, sports, etc.,) in place of him. God gives us flavorful food to remind us that we have tasted and seen his goodness. He gives us beautiful sunrises and sunsets to show us his splendor and beauty. He gives us mountains to show us his greatness and majesty, and he gives us oceans so we can know his infinite grace and mercy. As children, we learned what the color yellow was by looking at bananas and the color red by looking at firetrucks. In the same way, we know God's goodness because we have experienced the good things that he has given us.

My wife and I enjoy giving presents to our children on Christmas morning. We love seeing their faces light up as they tear through the wrapping paper and announce their gifts out loud. We want our children to enjoy their presents because we want them to know how much we love them. We give them gifts as expressions of our love for them, and God does the same for us. He enjoys giving us good things because he loves us and because these gifts point us to him.

(margin handwritten note: How is God good to us?)

Every time we are about to indulge in something fun as a family, I like to voice a prayer of thankfulness so that my children know it was God who gave us the good things we enjoy. We don't thank him because he is a genie who gives us what we want. We thank God for good things because those things remind us that the greatest treasure is God himself. The good things he gives us are signposts that point to his goodness. God is good to us not only because of the gifts he gives but also because his love is committed to making sacrifices on our behalf. Yes, we want to enjoy comfort, but sometimes comfort is the enemy of growth. And God is not afraid to sacrifice our temporary comfort for what is ultimately best for us. He is willing to take us through the fire to forge us into what we were made to be; because that is what is best for us.

My son Colin, who is three, will often make requests that I simply cannot (in good conscience) grant him. He recently stood in front of the freezer at eight o'clock in the morning and asked for a popsicle. Though the cereal I was trying to offer him was equally unhealthy, I held my ground that he should not have dessert for breakfast. I said "no." He cocked his head with a look of disbelief that I would not succumb to his cuteness as he demanded that he be given a popsicle for breakfast. As he angrily cried, running down the hall to his room, I was reminded of the similarities between Colin's relationship with me and our relationship with God. How often do we make our demands to God and get angry when we don't get the answer we want? We turn away from him constantly and disobey him repeatedly, yet God's love for us is unwavering. He is committed to what is best for us because he is committed to loving us. Though we may not always understand what God is doing, and though at times we may look to him with anger or disbelief, we must not forget that our wisdom compared to God's is like a three-year-old's. We can behold God's love for us and trust that he knows what is best.

Because he loved us first, we can wholeheartedly love him in return (1 John 4:19). Loving God means that we love him more than we love his toys. We seek to know him more, and we strive to obey his commands and live within his design. We bow to his Word, even when it doesn't make sense right away. Loving God means that we desire to be committed to him in the way that he is committed to us. We enter this commitment with him and give him priority above everything else, even when it is hard to do.

I love my wife and six beautiful children. I desire to spend time with them and give them good things. If I want to show love to my family in a moment, I can give my wife a big hug or take her to dinner. I can play checkers with my kids or take them to get an ice cream cone. But showing our love to God looks a little different. Jesus said, "If you love me, keep my commands" (John 14:15). His commands are summarized by loving God with all our heart, soul, and strength and loving our neighbor as ourselves.

Love people

As we drink in from God's love, we can respond by loving him in return through caring for the orphans and the widows. A selfless act of kindness to the poor or the needy is an act that is done unto God. This is the way that we show our love to him.

"Truly I tell you, whatever you did for one of the least of these brothers and sisters of mine, you did for me." – Matthew 25:40 (NIV)

God's love transforms us into lovers. It's not about the religious things we do or don't do. It's about love. Yes, we may go to church out of our love for God, but it is possible to go to a church gathering without ever putting these things into practice (Ezekiel 33:31-32). The way that we show our love to God is by loving people.

"And he has given us this command: Anyone who loves God must also love their brother and sister." – 1 John 4:21 (NIV)

We are called to love our brother and our sister. We are not called to love them when it is convenient or when they love us in return. Our love is not contingent upon whether it is reciprocated or not. Our love for others is rooted in our love for God. We love because it is who we are and what we do as children of God. Anyone can love their friends, but only the love of God in us can cause us to love our enemies as well. The love that we are called to is not based on the merit or the personality of the person we are loving. It is based on the love of God that is in us.

In 1 Corinthians 13, the Apostle Paul puts some flesh on what love actually looks like.

"Love is patient, love is kind. It does not envy, it does not boast, it is not proud. It does not dishonor others, it is not self-

seeking, it is not easily angered, it keeps no record of wrongs. Love does not delight in evil but rejoices with the truth. It always protects, always trusts, always hopes, always perseveres." – 1 Corinthians 13:4-7 (NIV)

These qualities have never been embodied perfectly except in one person, and that was Jesus. If you were studying his life for the definition of love, you could arrive at the same list of attributes found in 1 Corinthians 13 or Psalm 15. This kind of love always requires sacrifice. It gives of oneself for the good of someone else. This kind of love looks like pursuing justice, correcting the oppressor, defending the rights of the fatherless, pleading the widow's cause, and caring for the poor (Job 31:23, Isaiah 1:16-17). Jesus didn't die to get something from you. He died to get you. That's love. And when we are filled with this love, we won't just give to charity because we can write it off on our taxes, and we won't lay down our preferences just to make everyone think we are nice. We will love for the benefit of others, not self, because that's what Jesus did for us.

"What does love look like? It has the hands to help others. It has the feet to hasten to the poor and needy. It has eyes to see misery and want. It has the ears to hear the sighs and sorrows of men. That is what love looks like." – Augustine of Hippo

The most loving thing we can do for any human is to care for that person's soul; not just for physical needs and not just spiritual needs, but all of it. Though spiritual needs are more important than the physical, both are important, nonetheless. If we look at the ministry of Jesus as our example, we see that in each of the miracles he performed there was a physical and a spiritual need that was met. In the feeding of the five thousand, he filled the bellies of hungry people while teaching them that he was the true bread of life. He brought physical healing to the lame and the blind and then told them to "Go and sin no more." Jesus could have chosen one or the other, but he always addressed both. The love of God in us does not only care for the physical needs of the broken but also the spiritual needs. And the effect of physically demonstrating love for those who haven't earned it can often result in the awakening of their faith.

Caring for the physical needs of someone while neglecting the spiritual needs is like trying to make that person feel comfortable while he or she is unwittingly running towards the edge of a cliff. This ideology embodies one part of the person's needs but completely abandons the other. Is this really love at all? On the other hand, caring for one's spiritual needs while disregarding the physical needs often lacks favorable results. How can people be expected to believe that we have their best spiritual interest in mind when we are unwilling to tend to their most evident physical needs? You've probably seen a curmudgeon street preacher holding a sign on the street that says, "Turn or burn." While he might mean well, this saving message of repentance lacks many of the attributes of love described in 1 Corinthians 13; thus, creating a polarizing effect to the saving message of the gospel. This is not love. True love embraces both the physical and the spiritual needs.

When I am in the beginning stages of planting a garden, I don't carelessly throw seeds into the rocky soil and hope for the best. I remove the rocks. I care for the seedlings. I nurture them and water them but not too much. I fend off the birds and the critters. This is an ongoing process, not a one-time deal. And while some plants grow quickly and start producing fruit, others take much longer to mature.

Sometimes the plants that get the most care produce the least amount of fruit. This is just a part of gardening. The street preacher, who gracelessly demands repentance, is like the gardener who throws the seeds on rocky soil and hopes for the best. But true love will demonstrate care and protection while the roots are invisibly growing. True love welcomes interruptions to its comfort with no profit in return and doesn't let the fear of rejection inhibit the truth from being shared.

Jesus modeled what it looks like to be full of grace and truth. He showed kindness and goodness but didn't shy away from the truth. He wasn't one-half grace and one-half truth. He embodied both of them fully. As a parent, I understand this paradigm. I desire to speak kindly to my children all the time, but when they run towards the road, my kindness sounds more like an angry bellow. I'm not being unkind by yelling at them when they are running towards the road; but at that moment, kindness looks more like a cry of desperation. True kindness at that moment is not soft-spoken; it is boisterous. However, the opposite is also true. If I were to raise my voice at one of my children simply because that child did not clean up after eating his lunch, that would not be a demonstration of kindness, but rather a sign of impatience and frustration. True love is both gracious and truthful. The two are not pitted against each other, and to do so would be a false dichotomy.

If I were to take my wife to a fine restaurant for dinner, and mid-way through the dinner, she looked up at me with food stuck between her teeth, the most loving thing for me to do would be to make her aware of it. Disrupting the magic of the evening for a brief moment to give her this news would be something that I would not want to do. It would feel as though I were insulting her. However, true love would embody kindness and truthfulness at the same time.

We are called to seek justice, love mercy, and walk humbly with God (Micah 6:8). If we are not careful, we will take this imperative to assume the role of judge and jury in social justice issues and choose who gets justice and who gets mercy. We will see one person as a victim and another as an oppressor with little to no margin for gray area. The temptation is to seek justice against the oppressor and show mercy to the oppressed. After all, this is the most logical understanding of the concept. However, if we show justice to the oppressor, does this mean that we don't love mercy? And if we show mercy to the oppressed, should we assume that this person is not responsible for even the smallest infringement? How can we cast a judgment without knowing the hearts of each party involved, especially in a day of spin teams and media sensationalism?

What if, instead, we were to seek justice and love mercy at the same time for the same person? Is this not what God has done for us? We were dead in our sins as his enemies. We were deserving of the full weight of justice to be brought upon us. But God was rich in his mercy that even when we were dead, he brought us to life (Ephesians 2:4-6). God showed us justice and mercy at the same time by sacrificing his son to take the penalty of death we deserved. Yes, we want to cry for justice where there is injustice; but are we also willing to show mercy? Love intentionally takes the short end of the stick. Love says, "I will die so you can live." Love does not sacrifice mercy for justice or justice for mercy; it sacrifices itself for both.

The signs of someone who drinks from the fountain of living water manifest themselves through love. The love that filled us and brought us to life does not stop in us; it seeps out of us into our words and our actions. This love is contagious. Loved people love people. This same principle is true for all of our relationships.

Christ (the Groom) demonstrated his love for us (the bride) by laying down his own life in our place. Successful relationships are born out of selflessness and sacrifice — expecting nothing in return. This may seem counterintuitive, but it is the way our Maker intends for us to interact with each other. We were not designed only for relationships that benefit us, but for relationships that benefit from us. Love does not keep score. "I cleaned the house, I changed the diapers, and I paid the bills. What have you done?" This would be an example of what keeping score in a marriage might look like. You might feel like the sole giver in a relationship and that you deserve something more than you are currently receiving, but this mindset is born out of your brokenness—not out of your original design as an image-bearer.

Most secular counsel will tell you to drop the relationships that don't benefit you in some way. Culture will tell you to cancel them. But if we are to reflect the way that God showed his love toward us while we were sinners, then we will love those who benefit us least. Love will always require sacrifice from us. And whether someone deserves our love is irrelevant to the fact that we were designed to show it to them.

"This is how God showed his love among us: He sent his one and only Son into the world that we might live through him." – 1 John 4:9 (NIV)

CHAPTER 6

A NEW SONG

Along with a new identity and purpose comes a new song—a new soundtrack for life. When we were grafted into the family of God as new creatures, adopted into the living vine of Jesus, God put a new song in our hearts. This is a song of thankfulness and praise—a song of deliverance and freedom—a song that cannot be silenced. As children of the living God, we've learned a new melody. We live by the soundtrack of God's purpose and not our own. Once we marched to the beat of pride and selfishness, but now we dance to the rhythm of his love.

"He put a new song in my mouth, a hymn of praise to our God. Many will see and fear the Lord and put their trust in him." — Psalm 40:3 (NIV)

Oftentimes, when we think of the word "worship," we think about singing together with the church. We refer to singing as "worship," and we call our church songs

Our life is one long Song! What are the lyrics.

"worship music." There are more than four hundred references to singing in the Bible, many of which are direct commands. But God did not command us to sing without also giving us a reason to sing. There is a connection between worship and singing, but what is it? What exactly is the role of music when it comes to worship?

A Language of the Heart

The God of the universe who formed planets, stars, mountains, and canyons is the same God who created the sounds of thunder, stampedes, ocean waves, and chirping crickets. The rhythm of trees clapping their hands and the melodies of birds singing their songs express the unparalleled musicianship of the greatest composer of all time—God himself.

God is a musical being. He does not just enjoy music; he created it. He established the science of sound waves and audio frequencies, and he crafted all the raw materials used to make the musical instruments we enjoy. The God who created music formed us in his image, and he has woven music and singing into the fiber of our being. This musical God, who created us in his likeness, sings over us like a father singing over his children to calm us and rejoice over us (Zechariah 3:17). Musicians who make music with their voice or some other instrument mirror the very image of their Creator every time they create.

Though not all people are good at singing, most can sing, because it is the way we were made. Scientists have found that music stimulates more parts of the brain than any other human function. Music moves us. When the sound of music reaches the ear, it literally vibrates our eardrums and moves us. It causes us to feel deeply. Music has a unique way of touching us both physically and spiritually. So, why did God give music such an important part of human design?

The relationship that God wishes to have with us is not one devoid of emotion, but one of love, passion, and desire. God wants more than your mind and your obedience; he wants your heart. He wants all of you. He wants you to love and desire him more than anything else. And music is the language of the heart. It can penetrate the heart in ways that nothing else can. This is why the act of singing songs to God is often referred to as worship.

Singing and worship are both expressions of the heart; however, not all singing is worship and not all worship is singing. If we are merely singing songs to God while serving another master, we are no different from a man who tells his wife he loves her while sleeping with another woman. This kind of singing is not worshiping at all. To God, this kind of heartless singing is nothing more than a noise he wishes to silence (Amos 5:23). It would not be accurate to use "singing" and "worship" interchangeably for this very reason. Though it is possible to sing without worshiping, it is impossible to worship without singing. Worship includes willful obedience, and we are commanded to sing. Therefore, true worship will always be accompanied by a song. The heart drives our passions and emotions; so, it is no wonder that the God who desires our heart tells us to sing.

Music is a language that transcends all languages. Even if people of different languages cannot communicate with each other through words, they can understand the language of music. Music is like a delivery service that sends messages of emotion to and from the heart. It serves as a way of expressing the emotions that we feel, and there is a soundtrack to every human emotion. You could listen to a cartoon with your eyes closed and make an educated guess as to what was happening simply by listening to the soundtrack. The music would suggest if the scene was expressing happy, sad, suspenseful, or inspirational emotions. This same soundtrack could also have the power to create these emotions for the listener if they were not present already. For example, a minor chord may evoke mystery or suspense while a major chord might resolve tension. Music has a unique way of affecting our emotions and causing us to feel one way or another, and emotions have more power in our lives than we might even know.

In 1 Samuel 16:14-23, King Saul was tormented by an evil spirit. He requested for a skilled musician, David, to come and play a stringed instrument similar to a harp so that he would feel better. Whenever David played music, it would calm Saul's spirit and do exactly what he had hoped. Music has the power to greatly influence the way we feel, and the way we feel impacts the way we act.

A Harvard study observing the components of human decision-making concluded that emotions constitute powerful and predictable drivers of decision-making. In other words, you may credit logic and deductive reasoning for most of the decisions you make in your life, but studies show that in many cases it's our emotions that drive us to the decisions we make. It can be difficult to deny that "gut-feeling" or "pit in your stomach." Though we may not be able to articulate or substantiate why we feel a particular way, that doesn't always discredit those feelings. We might be inclined to turn down an offer on something because we didn't "have a peace about it." Many people give more weight to their feelings than to the facts that they have.

But emotions alone are not reliable for discerning what is true; because other things are contributing to our emotions, as well, such as hormones or false presuppositions. Unbalanced chemicals in the body can impact the way you feel, and these are not always in line with what is true. Just because you feel like you are good at something doesn't mean that you are actually good at it. And just because you feel well doesn't necessarily mean that there is not some underlying illness. So, it makes sense that emotions that are aligned with the truth are good, but emotions that oppose the truth need to be rooted out.

"Next to the Word of God, music deserves the highest praise. The gift of language combined with the gift of song was given to man that he should proclaim the Word of God through music." – Martin Luther

Music is a powerful tool for centering the heart because it has direct access to the heart's vault. The songs we sing help to form our worldview and shape the way we think of and interact with God. They catechize us. Songs are like sermons that get stuck in your head.

\\ *"So what shall I do? I will pray with my spirit, but I will also pray with my understanding; I will sing with my spirit, but I will also sing with my understanding." – 1 Corinthians 14:15 (NIV)* \\

This is why it is so important that the theology of our songs is biblically sound. When you are sad and down because of the shame from your past sin, you can sing the songs of redemption to remember that Jesus paid it all. When you are fearful of life's circumstances, songs of God's greatness remind us that he is bigger than our fears. These melodies can drown out the whispers of the accuser and change the way we feel. Songs can call out to our drifting emotions and anchor them back to what is true. The Word, coupled with music, stirs affections and hides truths in our hearts. Singing unites our hearts, minds, and bodies together. This is why we are instructed to enter the Lord's gates with singing (Psalm 100:4); because he doesn't just want our minds, he wants all of us – totally fixed on him.

An Instrument of Harmony

In Exodus 15, after God delivered his people from Pharaoh and his army, the first thing they did together was sang a song of praise to God. They sang of his greatness, majesty, and power; and recounted their victory with shouts of joy. The exodus was a foretelling of a greater salvation to come — our salvation. When we gather as a church in the name of Jesus — the one who conquered death with death to bring us life — we have a greater song to sing than they did back then. Our rescue is one that is eternal. Though the greatest version of our song will be at the final return of Jesus when people of every tribe, tongue, and nation sing "Worthy is the Lamb," we demonstrate a picture of heaven every time we gather with other believers to sing praises.

The act of singing has implications of unity that are unparalleled to any other human action. Singing demands unity of the heart, mind, and body; and when people sing together, their souls are unified with one another in this holistic way. Singing together makes us vulnerable and often makes us feel uncomfortable, but maybe that's the point. The church of Jesus is a body of believers that has been called into unity (1 Corinthians 12:27). Each member makes up a part of the body, and for the body to function properly it must be unified and fully aligned in Christ. When the church comes together to sing songs to Jesus, it is recharged and re-unified to be a healthy, functional body. When we come together to sing, we grow in our bond of unity with

Jesus and one another. We are united in thankfulness, passion, and mission.

"Therefore, since we are receiving a kingdom that cannot be shaken, let us be thankful, and so worship God acceptably with reverence and awe," – Hebrews 12:28 (NIV)

As we sing together, we are reminded that we belong to something bigger; that living for his kingdom is so much better than living for our own kingdoms. We are reminded that we are not alone on this journey. As a worship leader, one of the greatest joys of singing from the stage is looking out and seeing the faces of people I know and love, knowing that we are all in this together. I have my struggles and so does everyone else in the room. I have my burdens and so does everyone else. But there is one who is greater than all of our struggles and burdens combined. People of every age, ethnicity, and background gather with one thing in common: we are all sinners saved by the grace of God. Some were saved from lifestyles of reckless addiction, while others were saved from self-righteous piety. Yet, all of us, collectively, are united in thankfulness to God when we sing. We sing to remember who God is, what he has done for us, and what is yet to come. This leads us to thankfulness. This leads us to joyful praise and celebration. Thankfulness for what he has done and the promise of what is yet to come is what leads us to acceptable worship (Hebrews 12:28, Romans 12:1).

♪ Acceptable and reasonable worship is nothing less than giving over your entire being to God as a sacrifice of praise in response to what he has done for you. Your body was born from the seed of sinful Adam, but if you have accepted the gift of Christ, then your spirit was born from the seed of Jesus. Therefore, you must choose one by sacrificing the other. This might sound confusing and may cause you to question where you stand in the sight of God, but if you struggle with this battle, then that is a good sign. For if there were no battle between the spirit and the flesh at all, then there would be no evidence of the Spirit's presence; because, by nature, you were born of the flesh. What does this have to do with singing? We are fighting a spiritual battle. Singing is a deeply profound spiritual weapon against the powers of fear and idolatry. Singing is an act of repentance and recommittal to God.

"Through Jesus, therefore, let us continually offer to God a sacrifice of praise – the fruit of lips that openly profess his name. And do not forget to do good and to share with others, for with such sacrifices God is pleased." – Hebrews 13:15-16 (NIV)

As we sing together to the one who laid down his life for us, we are joyfully committing to laying down our own lives for our neighbors as an offering of praise to him. Our odious sins of selfishness and greed are laid on the altar. Our hearts sing. Our lips sing. And the fruit of our singing lips ripens into acts of love, kindness, and generosity towards others. When we sing, we stir our affections and emotions towards God and reset our worship back to its rightful place; considering ways to spur each other on in love and good works (Hebrews 10:24). As the physical act of individuals' singing unites hearts and actions together, the body of Christ sings to unite the heart of loving Jesus with the action of loving others. Let us not underestimate the power of singing praises to God with each other.

PART 3
TRANSFORMED BY WORSHIP

CHAPTER 7

RHYTHMS OF WORSHIP

When I was a kid, one of my greatest sports-heroes was Michael Jordan (me and every other kid in America). I can remember watching him score the winning jump-shot in Game 6 of the 1998 NBA Finals against Karl Malone and the Utah Jazz. I spent most of my summer afternoons at Montague Park in Santa Clara, playing street ball with my friends. If I wasn't at the park playing basketball, I was at home practicing my jump-shot in my backyard or playing one-on-one with one of my brothers. I wanted to be just like Mike. I wore a wristband on my left forearm and a pair of Jordan-wannabe's that looked almost exactly like Jordan's shoes. If I wasn't watching the Bulls, I was watching shows like "Michael Jordan's Playground" or "Come Fly with Me." I was a fanatic. My admiration for Michael Jordan moved me to want to be more like him. The more I studied him, the more obvious it was that I was trying to be just like him. I would even sing the song from the old Gatorade commercial— "If I could be like Mike."

This is how worship works.

Behold and Respond

Worship starts with beholding and leads to becoming. The more clarity and depth that comes to our vision leads to greater heights of transformational response. Worship is a lot like Newton's third law of motion: "For every action, there is an equal and opposite reaction." We inhale; we exhale. We take in visions and pour out proportionate responses. If we behold something worthy of glory, we will respond with glorious praise. Worship is seeing what is ultimate and responding with sacrifice. It is giving up what is important for what is most important. Worship says, "That one thing is going to fulfill me; therefore, I will give everything else to have it."

When you think about worship as being the response to an ultimate revelation, there is an essential component for worship to happen; there must be a revelation. It is beholding God and his goodness that fuels our worship. So, to have healthy worship, our hearts must be fueled by a daily dose of seeing the sovereign King on his throne. The health of our body relies on eating the right food every day. And the health of our worship is no different. We need daily exposure to Jesus, the bread of life, to be the food for our souls.

In the like manner, when we think of good health, we don't only think about diet; we also consider our physical activity and exercise. We go to the gym to work out, or we go for walks in the park. If we are not careful in this day of being sedentary in front of a computer screen all day, we will go the entire day without the physical exercise our body needs to remain healthy. Obedience to Jesus' greatest command is the outworking of our worship. It's what we were made to do, and without it, we are unhealthy.

If we are to live a life that models after that of Jesus' life, then we must keep a steady rhythm of beholding and becoming. It is beholding Jesus that fuels us with the desire and the power to worship him rightly. And though the desire to become more like him may be a natural response to the revelation of God's love, being fruitful does not come without effort. A desire does not equal an action. In other words, my desire to go to the gym doesn't equate with my going to the gym. If I have a gym membership but do not go to the gym, then I cannot say that I exercise. If you had the desire to eat food because your stomach was growling, you would not likely confuse the desire to eat with the action of eating. They are not the same thing. One leads to the other; it does not stand in as a replacement. Worshiping God and examining his love for you will undoubtedly fill you with a desire to walk in the Spirit by loving other people, but the desire does not automatically cause you to love people. It takes intentionality to walk in the Spirit. It takes both the discipline of renewing your mind to see the goodness of God and the discipline of creating margin into your life to be able to help those in need. True worship is a commitment both to pursue visions of God and to walk in obedience to him.

We are what we worship. What goes into our hearts is what will come out of us, and what we worship is what we will image. If we drink in from God's love, his love should flow out of us. However, if we plant a seed in the ground and set a boulder over it, the plant will never flourish. We must implement healthy rhythms of keeping the love of Jesus before us regularly, as well as rhythms of working out our good works as a response. A life of fruitfulness looks like a healthy rhythm of intake and output, of continual beholding and becoming. There needs to be a reliable irrigation system that feeds our souls with the motivational and transformational power of God's love. And there needs to be disciplines ensued to promote loving our neighbor.

Before Jesus ascended to heaven after the resurrection, he gave his disciples a command known to believers as the "Great Commission." But before the disciples were commanded to do anything, they first *saw* Jesus and *worshiped* him. It was beholding a resurrected Jesus that fueled their confidence in his Spirit's power. It was beholding the Savior who had laid down his life for them that fueled their desire to lay down their lives for others. It was beholding Jesus that led to their worshiping Jesus, and it was their worshiping Jesus that led to the joyful obedience of going.

"And when they saw him they worshiped him, but some doubted. And Jesus came and said to them, "All authority in heaven and on earth has been given to me. Go therefore and make disciples of all nations, baptizing them in the name of the Father and of the Son and of the Holy Spirit, teaching them to observe all

that I have commanded you. And behold, I am with you always, to the end of the age." – Matthew 28:17-20 (ESV)

Sight Without Vision

There is a myth that exists in some parts of Christianity that abstinence equals holiness. That if we abstain from evil, we will be good; or if we don't indulge in certain, sinful things, then we will be counted as "righteous." But this is neither consistent with the Scriptures nor with logic. It's not just about what we avoid, but also what we ingest that determines our outcome. We are transformed by what we consume; not just by what we don't consume. We are defined by what we do; not by what we don't do. Though Christians should abstain from certain things, we must not equate this to spiritual fruit.

"Nothing outside a person can defile them by going into them. Rather, it is what comes out of a person that defiles them." – Mark 7:15 (NIV)

For example, I know that herbicides will kill plants. However, avoiding herbicides will not guarantee healthy, fruitful plants; it simply means they will escape death by herbicide. If I want healthy plants, I need to nourish the plants with proper soil, light, and care. So, avoiding one terrible thing does not guarantee a positive outcome. If we want a plant to produce fruit, then it needs to open up and receive the water and let the sunlight in; because these are the only things that can produce the desired result. The same is true for us. Avoiding certain sins is not the same thing as being a successful human or a good Christian. Though I am by no means advocating that a sinful lifestyle is acceptable, I am simply making the point that godly transformation comes from drinking from the right source and growing in the light of the sun.

Transformation requires vision, and vision requires light. In the same way that light enters the window of our physical eyes through the cornea, God's light enters our soul through our heart's eye — through beholding. Worship is our response to beholding the greatest revelation on which we fix our heart's eye, but there is a giant veil covering the eyes of the proud. No light can shine into a proud heart because the veil is thicker than the blackout curtains of a hotel room. Pride is something that God not only despises but also opposes. Pride is the preoccupation with self; it contorts the heart's eye to look inward at itself, prohibiting true light from coming in. It is a result of misfired worship — the fruit of idolatry.

Fruitfulness looks like laying down oneself for the benefit of somebody else, and pride looks like propping up self at the expense of somebody else. Pride turned heaven's anointed angel into the devil, and it is what caused Eve to be deceived in the garden. Under the weed of every sin is the ugly root of pride. But when we turn to the Lord in humility, the veil is removed from our eyes and we are able to see the light. When we look to created things instead of the Creator of all things for security, comfort, or fulfillment, it's like we are crimping the hose of God's living water. But when we turn to him in repentance, there is a surge of the Holy Spirit's transformational power that washes over us and changes us. Humility might be associated with weakness by the world's standard, but in God's economy, we are made strong when we become weak. In our humility and honesty, we can access the power that makes us alive and free. In our humility, we can see the things that give us life.

"But whenever anyone turns to the Lord, the veil is taken away. Now the Lord is the Spirit, and where the Spirit of the Lord is, there is freedom. And we all, who with unveiled faces contemplate the Lord's glory, are being transformed into his image with ever-increasing glory, which comes from the Lord, who is the Spirit." – 2 Corinthians 3:16-18 (NIV)

I heard the story once of a mom and her two young boys who were vacationing on the white sandy beaches of Florida. They were enjoying a day in the sun. She was enthralled in a book while her two boys took turns burying each other in the sand just a few feet away. As the tide came in, the mom and two boys were caught off guard by a wave that seemed to come out of nowhere, washing over the youngest of the two sons buried alive under the wet sand. A vacation in paradise instantly turned into a mother's worst nightmare. As she frantically began digging in search of her son, a man came out of nowhere and started digging alongside her. Moments later, the man pulled the boy out of the sand and performed CPR. His heroic act on the beach saved a life that day, and the little boy lived to tell the story.

Years later, the mom and her son were still in contact with this man who saved the boy's life. They send him cards on his birthday and at Christmas time because they are forever grateful and in his debt for what he did on the beach that day. The thankfulness and appreciation that filled the mother of that boy came from experiencing a gift of kindness and love, unlike any other one she had ever received. This revelation would not be one she would ever forget, and it would lead her to a desire to express her thankfulness at any cost.

I suppose the mother of the rescued boy will never forget about what happened on the beach that day. She may not think of it every day, but she will always live in the light of that reality. I am sure that whenever she is reminded of the terrible vision of her son buried beneath the sand, she is moved to hold him a little tighter and hug him a little longer, knowing that she had almost lost him. When we catch a glimpse of what God did for us, it should shake us so hard that it dethrones anything else that may have been occupying the throne on our hearts. And though we may need reminding sometimes, a true understanding of God's love will not be something we forget so easily.

Many people, particularly in America, have heard the story of Jesus dying on the cross in our place, but most have not felt it in the same way that the mother of the rescued son felt that day on the beach. What Jesus did for us was an even greater rescue, yet we fail to see it. Perhaps the reason is that pride has prevented us from seeing just how badly our condition actually was. Maybe we saw ourselves as sick people who needed healing, instead of the reality that we were dead people who needed resurrection. If our understanding of what Christ did for us elicits nothing more than a dignified courtesy clap, then it is likely we didn't fully realize what he saved us from. If we truly understood what we were saved from and saw the glory of what we've been saved to, then our response would be true worship. It would not be, "What is the bare minimum?" but rather, "How can we give more?" (Romans 12:1).

The depth of our vision determines the height of our response. If we have a dimly lit vision of Jesus, then our response will be passivity towards him. But if we see a robust vision of Christ as the one who laid down his life for us, then our response will be sacrificially laying down our lives for others. Worship is not only beholding, and it is not only responding. It is not just seeing God, and it is not just obedience to him. True worship is the marriage of both.

If we don't desire to respond to Jesus with obedience, then it is likely we haven't truly *seen* him. If we don't desire to lift our voices in praise to God, it must be that we haven't heard his voice singing over us. If Jesus isn't our daily bread; it is because our bellies are full, and he isn't needed. If Jesus isn't our healer, it is because we are getting our fix elsewhere. If Jesus isn't our living water, it is because we are drunk with distractions and pleasure. If we do not forgive our neighbors for doing wrong to us, it must be that we have not experienced the forgiveness God extended to us. If we do not love our neighbor, it is because we have not grasped the greatness of God's love for us. As Hellen Keller said, *"The only thing worse than being blind is having sight but no vision."*

Paul the Apostle wrote a letter to the Ephesians, praying that they would be able to have the strength to comprehend the magnitude of God's love for them (Ephesians 3:17-19). His prayer was not for them to have the strength to do better or try harder. His prayer was for them to have the strength to grasp the greatness of God's love so it would fill them with the fullness of God. Do you know what happens when something is filled with the fullness of something else? It starts to spill over with that thing. But we cannot overflow with something until we, ourselves, are first filled; and this begins with capturing a greater vision. As Paul prayed, may we have the power to grasp the greatness of God's love; because only when we've experienced the love of God in its fullness will we truly see one who is worthy of radical worship that produces a life of fruitfulness.

Rhythms of Beholding

There is a direct correlation between beholding and being motivated. For example, as a kid, you might have been motivated to sell candy bars after seeing the magazine full of prizes that you would get for selling the most candy. Or as an adult, you might be motivated to go to the gym because you have a favorite pair of jeans you want to fit into. Either way, beholding a vision of something in the future might cause you to say "no" to one thing as a way of saying "yes" to something else. This future vision motivates you in the present.

The idea of eating ice cream in place of eating vegetables might sound pleasing to your tastebuds at first, but once the bellyaches become a nuisance, the gratification of indulging in sweets would wear off. The choice of good health would be a better decision in the long run than the choice of instant pleasure that brings nothing more than bellyaches and cavities. God has illuminated his path to be the only road to joy and abundant life, yet we choose the backroads of pain and emptiness when we veer off to seek our own pleasures. God has offered us the richest of meats and finest of wines, yet when we choose our way over his way, we are choosing to eat with the pigs instead (Isaiah 25:6). There is a future vision that should inform our present choices, and we need to see that God's way is better than our way; that his riches are greater than our riches. We need to see that his grace is greater than our sins and that his love is bigger than our fear.

In Isaiah 6, the prophet Isaiah tells of a vision where he saw the Lord seated on his throne in his temple. He saw seraphim angels flying around him, singing, "Holy, Holy, Holy." This revelation of God's greatness revealed to Isaiah that he was unworthy and unclean; therefore, inhibiting him from even joining in with the angels' song. But then God sent an angel to purify Isaiah's lips with burning coals from the fire, and this revelation elicited praise and a willingness to go wherever the Lord said to go (Isaiah 6:1-8). Isaiah's

YOU ARE WHAT YOU WORSHIP

exposure to God's greatness led him to see that his greatest need was a savior. And the vision of God's goodness would lead him to the ultimate act of worship through joyful obedience. It was beholding that led Isaiah to worship, and it was his worship that produced the fruit of obedience.

A true revelation of God will leave an imprint on our hearts and minds that demands our attention. In fact, when the immensity of God and his character are put on display, there is a certain level of awareness and sobriety that is compulsory. Throughout the Old Testament, whenever the presence of God was made known to man, it was usually a terrifying experience (2 Samuel 6:7, Exodus 33:18-20). The presence of God is not something we can casually experience. Either we fear God, or we fear something else. Beholding God is the first step to fearing him, and fearing him rightly is the first step to having wisdom (Proverbs 9:10). *fear of God?*

When we think of fear, we typically think of unhealthy fear. We think of anxiety, panic, and stress. But God has not given us the spirit of this kind of fear. This fear undermines God's sovereignty. However, there is a fear that is good and healthy; a kind of fear that leads to worship.

Picture yourself standing on the roof of a skyscraper. The views from the top are breathtaking as you watch the sun setting over the city. The closer you get to the edge of the roof, the more aware you become of the danger of falling. There is an acute awareness of the distance between your feet and the edge of the roof. The gusts of wind cause you to take a few steps back as a precaution. Though you want to

114

stand tall to get a better view, you can't help but crouch down to keep your feet from tingling in fear. Although the altitude brings an awe-inspiring perspective, it also causes a heightened sense of focus—a fear. Neither the stunning views nor the present danger would elicit anything less than a sober mind and wide-open eyes. There is nothing foolish about fearing the edge of the roof. On the contrary—it would be unwise not to fear it. This kind of fear is wisdom. This kind of fear demands our full attention. This is how we must fear the Lord.

Every year our family takes a trip to the world's largest natural habitat zoo, which just happens to be minutes down the road from us in Asheboro, NC. Like most zoos, you can expect to see all types of animals, reptiles, and birds. But some animals are much more interesting to watch than others. As would be expected, our kids take the most interest in the animals that could eat them. They want to see the animals with sharp teeth and long claws. The snakes and spiders are interesting, and the elephants and monkeys are fun to watch, but nothing compares to standing a few feet away from a lion or a tiger. Why is this? I think it is because these are the animals that we fear the most. Fearing a lion is not a bad thing. It would be unwise not to fear a lion. Our whole family will stand and watch the lions longer than they will at any other animal exhibit, especially when the lions are most active (which seems to be rare sometimes). We fix our eyes on their awe-inspiring strength. We don't stand at the lion exhibit and look at the plants or the flowers surrounding it. We are locked in with the lions. If the rails and trenches were not between the lions and us, there is zero chance that we would still be standing there. This kind of fear points to the way we should fear God. C.S. Lewis wrote in his book, The Lion the Witch and Wardrobe:

"Aslan is a lion — the Lion, the great Lion." "Ooh," said Susan. "I'd thought he was a man. Is he-quite safe? I shall feel rather nervous about meeting a lion" "Safe?" said Mr. Beaver... "Who said anything about safe? 'Course he isn't safe. But he's good. He's the King, I tell you."

God is to be feared above all gods. He is not safe, but he is good. When we fear God, we will fix our eyes on him; just as we do to the lions at the zoo. When we fix our eyes on him, we will behold his greatness and his strength. His majesty and power will capture our gaze. And as we examine his love, it will bring us to our knees. When we fear God, it will lead to worship. When we fear him above man, then we will keep our eyes on him instead of on ourselves. Though we should fear God, we should no longer fear his wrath if we are hidden in Christ. God is not waiting to kick us when we fall. On the contrary, he longs to pick us up when we do. Fearing God leads us to examine him, and when we examine him, we see that his greatness and his goodness are better than everything else (Psalm 63:3). The vision of the greatness and goodness of God through Jesus is our single greatest daily need. Renewing our minds about who God is and what he's done for us is what fuels our worship and produces fruitfulness.

"Oh, magnify the Lord with me, and let us exalt his name together!" – Psalm 34:3 (ESV)

Before we can truly exalt the name of the Lord, we need to see him clearly. We need to put him under a microscope so that he is magnified before our eyes. We need to behold and see who he is and what he has done so that our worship will be fueled. Worship comes from seeing Jesus in all his power and glory. And fruit comes from abiding in God just as a root abides in water. Jesus is the tree, we are the branches, and his fruit comes out of us when we are filled with him. If we want to be fruitful, then we must abide in the vine daily (John 15:4). If beholding is the way in which we can begin to abide in him, then it is paramount for us to set disciplines and rhythms to see him.

One of the greatest rhythms that we can bake into our lives is prayerfully meditating on God's Word (Psalm 1:2). Romans 10:17 says that "Faith comes by hearing, and hearing by the Word of God." In the same way, we look to physical food for fueling our day, we can look to the Word to be our spiritual bread (Matthew 6:11). The Bible doesn't teach us only to read it, but also to meditate on it. For it is in meditating on the Scriptures that we can allow it to renew our minds.

The Holy Spirit rides on the words of the gospel, bringing the power of life to us (1 Corinthians 1:18). His power is packed inside the very words of what Jesus did for us on the cross, and it is the message of the gospel that renews our minds for transformation (Romans 12:2). When the Word of God gets into our minds, the Holy Spirit fills us with life and starts to rewire us back into our intended design, leading us to a life of fruitfulness. God's Word is like a mirror, and as we behold God through it, we begin to see the difference between who we are and who we were made to be.

"Anyone who listens to the word but does not do what it says is like someone who looks at his face in a mirror and, after looking at himself, goes away and immediately forgets what he looks like. But whoever looks intently into the perfect law that gives freedom, and continues in it – not forgetting what they have heard, but doing it – they will be blessed in what they do." – James 1:23-25 (NIV)

Without beholding, we will lack the power to become who God wants us to be. Trying to bear fruit on an empty tank is like trying to push a train up a hill. It is not only exhausting, but it is also unsustainable. The love of God is the fuel that moves us forward into our purpose, and there needs to be a steady rhythm of drinking from his love.

If the success of our jobs depended on waking up at a certain time every day, then we would discipline ourselves to set an alarm or two to wake us up in the morning. Most of us do this every day without giving it much thought. And if the life of a plant depended on seeing the light of the sun, then we would be sure to place our plants next to the window. These are things that need to happen; so, we make them happen. Since fulfilling our purpose of being fruit-bearing image-bearers only comes from true worship, and true worship only comes from beholding God's greatness and goodness, then it is only logical that we would not leave something so important to spontaneity or chance. This is not just a job or a plant; we are talking about the very purpose of our existence. We must be disciplined enough to set rhythms of spending time with Jesus. This is not about checking off a list of religious practices; it's about seeking God. And when we diligently seek him, we will find our purpose (Hebrews 11:6).

Rhythms of Response

Just as we need rhythms of beholding in our life, we also need rhythms of working out the fruit of the Spirit. Although it is the vision of God's love that fuels us, it still requires the discipline of creating margin into our life that allows us to put these things into practice so that we are not only worshiping in spirit but also in truth. It is impossible to be generous when we have empty pockets, and where there is no margin in our schedules, there is no chance of seizing the opportunities that present themselves in the midst of our busyness. True fruitfulness does not wait for convenient opportunities to arise; it creates them. It writes, "Love your neighbor" on the calendar, not only when you feel like it, but also when you don't.

Luke 8:15 teaches us to bear fruit with perseverance. This means we are to be fruit-bearers even when we don't have a desire to be. But disciplines produce desires, and desires produce disciplines. For example, most runners love running, but for the people who are first starting out as runners, this is not always the case. It takes the initial desire of becoming a runner to produce the disciplines that are needed for being a runner. And it takes the discipline of consistent running to produce the desire to keep running. Eventually, the desires and disciplines will sync together but not at first. Maybe you desire to learn a new language, or an instrument, or how to paint; for me, songwriting is a personal hobby and creative outlet. It has developed into a passion over the years, but it didn't start that way for me. In the past, I would only write when inspiration struck, which wasn't often. But I've learned from other, experienced veterans that songwriters should not wait for inspiration to come; they need to look for it. Successful songwriters discipline themselves to write several times per week, whether they are inspired or not. The discipline not only produces more songs, but it also produces more passion, experience, skill, and eventually more inspiration. The desire to be fruitful should lead us to set the proper disciplines.

"And let us not grow weary of doing good, for in due season we will reap, if we do not give up." — Galatians 6:9 (ESV)

It was Friday — my day off. I didn't have any plans on the calendar, and the kids were at school. Usually, I would take this time to do a project around the house or do some writing, but I lacked all motivation. I was tired and completely in my head. I wanted to do something meaningful, something significant that would make a difference. But all I could think about were my own feelings. What could I do for myself that would make me feel better? I stopped at Target to grab a few things, and as I was leaving, I walked through the parking lot to my car and said a prayer similar to this one. "God, please empty me of myself and let me walk in your Spirit." Just as I got into my car and started the engine, I noticed in my rearview mirror that there was a car behind me with the front hood open. I typically would have just backed out of my parking stall and drove back home, but all I could think at that moment was that the Spirit of God was answering my prayer by giving me an opportunity to walk in the Spirit. I had already spent time that morning abiding in the Spirit by reading my Bible, but now I had a chance to actually walk in it—to put it into practice and let the Holy Spirit take over my actions. After all, we are not only commanded to abide by the Spirit; we are also called to walk in it.

I got out of my car, pulled out my jumper cables, and proceeded to help Gary (the owner of the broken-down car) jump-start his car. It was as if God knew that I had nothing but time on my hands and wanted to see how far I was willing to go. I could tell that Gary's car battery was too far gone to be jump-started; so, I offered to call AAA for him before I left. Gary didn't understand why I would offer to do that, but that didn't keep him from taking up my offer. I called AAA and explained the situation to them, to which they replied, "We will be out in the next forty-five minutes."

But the real problem was that I would need to be there when they arrived to show them my membership identification. This moment of benevolence became much more inconvenient for me than I had anticipated, and the temptation of saying, "Sorry, hope you figure it out," was strong. But God kept reminding me that the sacrifice he made for me on the cross was much more inconvenient than sitting in a parking lot for forty-five minutes. So, I stuck around. Gary and I sat in the parking lot for forty-five minutes and got to know each other. After about twenty minutes of small talk, Gary asked me why I would sit around for almost an hour only to help a random stranger. I was able to share with him that Jesus did the same for me. I told him that I was broken down with nothing, and Jesus gave everything for me. I told him that I could show my love to Jesus in return by choosing to demonstrate that kind of love to him.

As AAA arrived, they hit me with the news that the free towing service only covered five miles of towing, and Gary lived about ten miles away. At this point, I had already committed to showing my love to Jesus through Gary, so I went into Target to pull out cash and proceeded to pay the cost of towing to the truck driver. I could tell the driver was confused by the relationship dynamic between Gary and me. He knew we were strangers and that I was paying for him, but he didn't understand what was happening. Gary and the tow truck driver drove off, and I haven't seen Gary since. But I can only imagine Gary getting into the truck with the driver and sharing with him the good news of the gospel that he had just heard from me. I don't share this story to toot my own horn; because, truthfully, I pass over these opportunities much more frequently than I seize them. But I can say from experience that one of the best ways to restore the joy of your salvation is to pursue opportunities to show love to people. There is nothing that makes you feel more alive than responding to God's love by sacrificially giving of yourself for the benefit of someone else. Maybe the reason it restores joy is that it's what we were truly designed to do in the first place, to love as we've been loved.

Creating margin and prayerfully seeking opportunities to show love to friends and strangers is one of the most life-giving and meaningful things we can ever do (Romans 12:1). And we must not neglect to show our love to those closest to us. Are there opportunities today to show love to your roommate, sibling, co-worker, or spouse? These are the people you do life with every day. And these are the greatest opportunities you have to put love into action. Christians often see familial relationships as a picture of God's love toward us. We see his kindness as a father who loves his children. We see his sacrifice as a husband who lays down his life for his bride. We see his selflessness as a friend who is closer than a brother. But do we see these same familial relationships as a way to reciprocate that love? Because Christ loved us enough to sacrifice everything for us, we can respond by doing these things for others. We can lay down our comfort for a brother or sister. We can love our spouse sacrificially. We can display selflessness to a roommate or friend. We can forgive the unforgivable.

"Therefore, I urge you, brothers and sisters, in view of God's mercy, to offer your bodies as a living sacrifice, holy and pleasing to God — this is your true and proper worship." — Romans 12:1 (NIV)

In view of God's mercy, respond with sacrificial living. This is the rhythm of true worship. We see what God did for us and respond by doing the same toward others. What did Christ do for us? How did he show mercy? This is where we take cues for the proper and reasonable way to respond to him. This is what true worship looks like.

CHAPTER 8

BEARING FRUIT

In the words of Anthelme Brillat-Savarin, "Tell me what you eat, and I will tell you what you are." This statement could be inverted and still be true. Tell me what you are, and I will tell you what you eat. And the same is true with worship. Tell me how you act, and I will tell you what you worship.

The fruit of being spiritually alive, also known as the fruit of the Spirit, is love, joy, peace, patience, kindness, goodness, faithfulness, gentleness, and self-control (Galatians 5:22-23). These are the things that flow out of someone who is spiritually living. Without evidence of these things, it is doubtful that there is life. We are reflectors of the image we worship. If these godly characteristics are not emanating from us, then we should take inventory of who or what is on the receiving end of our beholding. However, it is important to note a few things about this.

First, no trees produce fruit right away. What begins as a seed grows into a seedling, and then eventually after its roots have been established it will begin to produce. Fruit isn't immediate, but it is imminent.

Second, it is important to understand that while spiritual fruit may look like showing your neighbor patience or kindness, showing patience and kindness to your neighbor may not always be a result of spiritual growth. C. S. Lewis wrote a section in "Mere Christianity" about the difference in natural temperament and disposition from one person to the next. While one person may have the innate qualities of being patient and kind, another may start his journey in this life with the qualities of being impatient and unkind. When measuring the fruit in our lives, we should not compare one person to the next, but rather one person to his own starting point in these areas. A kind person may not be showing kindness out of spiritual renewal but out of his innate temperament; while another may have a naturally shorter fuse that is growing, even if only a little. This person should not look at his neighbor's patience and conclude that his fruit is not substantial enough. Instead, he should look at his current temperament as compared to the way it once was.

"By their fruit you will recognize them. Do people pick grapes from thornbushes, or figs from thistles? Likewise, every good tree bears good fruit, but a bad tree bears bad fruit." — Matthew 7:16-17 (NIV)

I can walk out to my garden right now and see that some of my plants have gone to be in plant heaven while others are still alive and well. I can tell these things simply by looking at their fruit. Some of my plants are bearing quite a bit of fruit, while others have stopped producing anything other than shriveled up leaves. There may be seasons in life where there is no evidence of fruit, and that may not always necessarily mean that the health of the plant is in decline. But generally, fruit *will* manifest if the plant is alive.

God's design for humanity is that we love God and love people. Love is not a side effect of being a Christian; it is the whole point. It is the fruit of being made in the image of the new Adam—Jesus. It is the evidence of being fully alive. The bumper stickers we put on the back of our minivans and the Bible verses we post on Facebook are fine, but we must not forget that it is by our love that people will know we are followers of Christ.

"By this all people will know that you are my disciples, if you have love for one another." — John 13:35 (ESV)

Faith and Works

There is a connection between faith and works that can be confusing, but it doesn't have to be. We were made for good works, but good works cannot make us alive. Works without faith are filthy rags, but faith without works is dead. Martin Luther said, *"We are saved by faith alone, but the faith that saves is never alone."*

In the story of the sinking island from chapter 4, no one ever claimed that walking onto the boat is what brought salvation. The glory of the rescue goes to the captain of the boat, not the people who were rescued. However, only the people who got on the boat were rescued, while everyone else was not. It was not walking onto the boat that brought salvation, but it was a result of faith that they walked onto the boat to receive their salvation. In the same way, it is not our works that save us, but it is our works that prove what our faith is in. Faith is not the opposite of works; it precedes our works. But faith without works is not faith at all.

"For as the body apart from the spirit is dead, so also faith apart from works is dead." – James 2:26 (ESV)

Let me illustrate this in another way. I am currently sitting in a chair. Before I sat down in this chair, I had faith that this chair would hold my weight. Believing that this chair would hold my weight does not mean that the chair is holding my weight. It only means that I believe it will hold my weight if I so choose to sit down in it. Once I choose to sit down, the chair will hold all the weight. All the work is being done by the chair, not by me. The chair gets credit for holding my weight.

Though faith begins in the mind, it does not stay in the mind. If faith in my mind never physically moves my body to sit down, then that faith is only a theory, not true faith. To say that you have faith in Jesus while not loving your neighbor can only mean one of two things: either you did not know that this is what Jesus was asking of you, in which case you can no longer use that excuse; or your faith in God is only a theory. If this is the case, then you are not worshiping in spirit AND truth. Faith always manifests itself in worship and action. As binary creatures, our spiritual faith will always have physical fruit. This fruit is the evidence of your worship. If we believe that true happiness is found in money, toys, and fame, then our actions will expose it. Having true faith in Christ will always be manifested through the fruit of the spirit. Always.

Test Yourself

"Examine yourselves to see whether you are in the faith; test yourselves. Do you not realize that Christ Jesus is in you — unless, of course, you fail the test?" – 2 Corinthians 13:5 (NIV)

In Exodus 15, after having endured four hundred years of oppression and abuse from Pharaoh and the Egyptians, the people of Israel sang their songs of freedom on the other side of the Red Sea. But this song of celebration was short-lived when they soon realized that they were stranded in the wilderness with nowhere to go. Though they were free from their slavery in Egypt, the wilderness caused them to doubt their freedom. They were still enslaved by their unbelief. The people of Israel would end up spending forty years in the wilderness. All of them, except for two, died in the wilderness and never even made it to the Promised Land. This is a part of the story that you probably don't hear as often. We like singing about the parting of the sea, but let's be real. They didn't make it to the Promised Land because of their unbelief (Hebrews 3:19). Sure, they believed that God had delivered them from their past slavery, but they didn't believe him with their future. They believed him enough to be rescued from Egypt but not enough to lead them out of the wilderness. They might as well have stayed in Egypt where at least they had food and shelter. Even though God never failed to provide for their needs, they still failed to take him at his word and walk in obedience.

wow !

In a similar way, Jesus came to the earth to deliver his people from the slavery of sin and death, and to lead us into a new heaven and earth where those things are but a memory. But before this new reality is fully realized, we must first endure our wilderness. What we often don't realize is that freedom from slavery is not a free ticket to the Promised Land; it is a ticket to the wilderness. The hard fact is that we are still in the wilderness and our faith is still being tested. Sometimes being in the wilderness can cause us to doubt our freedom. And the idea of going back into slavery doesn't always seem so bad. But if we could only see the beauty of the Promised Land, we would gladly forsake Egypt and endure the wilderness for it. If we only knew how wonderful it would be to be fully alive, we would be all too happy to endure the struggles of this temporary life. Yes, we are in the wilderness, but that does not mean freedom is presently unattainable. Our freedom is not contingent upon favorable circumstances. Even Paul and Silas were free in a prison cell.

In my experience of working in vocational ministry over the years, I've spoken to many professing Christians who have struggled at times to feel that their faith is genuine. They know in their minds that Jesus delivered them from their sins, but they struggle to feel like their faith is authentic and they don't know why. So, they go to church hoping to find the feeling of freedom, but it still feels like Egypt to them. The church tells them that if they believe in Christ that their sins are in fact covered and they are blameless in the sight of God. This helps a little, but by Monday or Tuesday, they fall back into the cycle of feeling shameful or empty, doubting the legitimacy of their freedom once again. But perhaps the reason for not feeling free in our wilderness is that we do not walk in obedience to Christ's commands.

If the greatest command is to love, then the greatest fracture in our brokenness is that we do not have love. The good news is that Jesus, filled with love, became broken for us so that we could become whole. Perhaps the reason we feel broken at times is that we were made for love and we do not have love, and maybe this is the reason we don't feel alive or free. 2 Peter 1:10 tells us to make every effort to confirm that we are truly alive in Jesus. Meaning, if life in Jesus produces love, then we should make every effort to prove that the love of Jesus is in us by demonstrating that love. This is how we can test the authenticity of our faith; because faith manifests in action. If we want to test our belief, we will exercise obedience to Jesus' greatest command. After all, the people of Israel did not enter the Promised Land because of their unbelief, which is to say, because of their disobedience. They did not believe God's promises; thus, they disobeyed his commands. So, it makes sense that if we want to see the fruit of our faith, we must be obedient to love.

If you want to test whether your faith is truly in Jesus, then trust his words by seeking opportunities to show love. Show patience to someone who might typically cause you to lose your temper. Be kind to someone who is not kind to you. Do something nice for someone without telling anyone else about it. Forgive the person who did something wrong to you. Go and seek out good for someone else at your own expense. These are the things that will make you feel alive because they are the things that a fully alive person does (Matthew 5-7). If you want to confirm that you are alive, then start acting alive; not out of your own power, but out of the Holy Spirit's power that comes from beholding God's love for you.

"Work hard to show the results of your salvation, obeying God with deep reverence and fear. For God is working in you, giving you the desire and the power to do what pleases him." – Philippians 2:12-13 (NIV)

Scientists have said that because of our procedural memory, riding a bike is something you never forget how to do. But what if you haven't ridden a bike in twenty-plus years and you are doubtful of this truth, yet you want to confirm that you indeed do still know how to ride a bike? How can one confirm this? Should you find people to talk to who will convince you that you can still ride a bike? Should you do the research and weigh the odds if you can or not? Should you join bike-riding Facebook groups or listen to biking podcasts? Of course not. This would be silly. If you want to know whether you can still ride a bike, then you should sit on the bike seat and start pedaling. It's that simple.

If you didn't feel like you were truly a Christian, even though you believed in your mind that you were, then I would tell you to confirm this truth by doing what a Christian does. Go and sin no more. In other words, swallow your pride and go seek out an opportunity to love someone, because that's what a Christian does. If we read all the books, listen to all the podcasts and sermons, sing all the worship songs, give our tithes and offerings, but do not have love, we are nothing (1 Corinthians 13, Amos 4:4-5).

What makes a runner a runner? Is it his affinity for "all things running"? Is it the shoes he wears, the food he eats, or the amount of running he watches on tv? No. Though a runner might do these things, there is only one thing that makes a runner a runner. And that is the fact that he runs. When he doesn't feel like a runner, there is no need to seek out a professional runner to convince him that he is one; he simply needs to feel the trail beneath his feet and the wind against his face to remember that he is a runner.

In this post-informational day in which we live, where it seems every decision that is made requires a spreadsheet of analytical research and data, I believe that we have taken the simplicity and purity of true worship and have twisted it into a convoluted, inferior substitute. What may have begun with pure intentions to worship God has resulted in doing everything but true worship. One side tells you to work harder and do more until you've driven yourself to the ground, while the other side tells you to slow down in the presence of God to the point of inactivity and mystical emotionalism. Our worship has become more about pursuing an experience than a person, and the end result is rootless wandering and exhaustion. The desire and will of God for our lives is not as complicated as we have made it. Meanwhile, God's Word still says, "Love God and love your neighbor." This is true worship.

If you believe in your heart that Jesus covered the cost of your sins, then your call is to "go and sin no more." Translation: If you accept Jesus' gift of love, then your response is to start loving. We can love God by looking for opportunities to show it. When God's love takes over our minds and our hearts, it develops a radar that causes us to become sensitive to the needs of those around us. God's love in us creates an opportunistic mindset to see people's needs around us as blank canvasses for painting pictures of God's love. The person on the side of the road that you help reaps the benefit of God's love in you. And this is the way God designed it all to work.

"We know that we have passed out of death into life, because we love the brothers. Whoever does not love abides in death" – 1 John 3:14 (ESV)

PART 4
EVERY DAY, WORSHIP

CHAPTER 9

SCATTERED

We gather with the church once per week to sing songs to God and build each other up in love and good works, but what about the other 99% of our week? How does true worship transform this part of our lives? We might be able to create margin in our schedules for serving the community and showing love to our neighbors, but what about the rest of our time? What about all the time spent at work, eating meals, going to the gym, and watching Netflix? Though the greatest command of Jesus is to love God and love our neighbors, it is not possible to spend every minute of our day dropping food off at the food bank and picking up groceries for your elderly neighbor.

Work

The average American spends most of their waking hours working a job. There isn't much choice in the matter. We must work to put a roof over our heads and food on our tables. So, where does work fit into the worship equation? The answer has to do with whose glory we work for.

The idea that working for God's kingdom and working at our jobs are two separate things with no overlap is a false dichotomy. Remember, we are physical and spiritual beings; so, everything we do has physical and spiritual implications. In other words, the physical work we do at our jobs can be done unto the Lord.

"Whatever you do, work at it with all your heart, as working for the Lord, not for human masters," – Colossians 3:23 (NIV)

God created the heavens and the earth to tell of his glory. His labor and creativity were servants of his glory. God told the stars to shine, and they did. And still today, the stars are declaring God's wonder and splendor. In John 9, Jesus healed a blind man so that the works of God might be displayed in him. God works for his glory, and so should we. When we worship the God who designs, creates, and works with passion for his own glory, we will see that the purpose of our work is also for his glory. God works hard, and he's more creative than all of us combined. He does it all for his own name's sake. We were designed for this as well. Working is what God created Adam to do in the Garden of Eden, even before the fall of man. We were made to work but not for our own glory. Our work is meant to be for his glory. What exactly does it look like to give God glory with your work? Consider this example.

Jeff works in the IT department at a large corporation. Whenever people have problems with their computers, Jeff is the guy they call to come and fix it. The company required every employee to install some new software that unintentionally crippled everyone's computers, causing their machines to operate slowly. The service requests started flooding in, and Jeff felt the urge to become overwhelmed with stress.

"Jeff, I need you to come and fix this right away. I have important deadlines to keep!" All eyes were on Jeff. Jeff could have very easily succumbed to the stress and lashed out with sharp replies, but this isn't the way he chose to respond. Jeff is a follower of Jesus. He isn't perfect, and on several occasions in the past, he has lost his temper. But Jeff decided that today he was going to trust in the sovereignty of God and accept the fact that everything happens for a reason. Jeff was going to respond to every single request with respect and honor, despite the ugly requests that had been made to him already.

Jeff kept his cool and was innovative enough to figure out a way to fix everyone's computers at the same time through the servers. He was the hero of the hour, and Jeff was thankful to God for this opportunity. Jeff's trust in God's sovereignty caused him to be patient and calm. Remembering God's patience and kindness toward Jeff, he modeled these things to the best of his ability through the kind email replies. Jeff's meek spirit led him to have enough mental capacity to form an innovative solution to the problem. The people who had sent condescending urgent requests to Jeff asked with bewilderment why he responded so politely. Jeff was able to share, "Because that's what God did for me."

Working hard with integrity, passion, skill, and innovation is a wonderful way to honor God with the talent he has given us while honoring and respecting those around us. These are the qualities that reflect the Creator of the universe. While many Christians might understand that God is glorified through our honesty and integrity, we must not forget that one of the greatest ways to bring God glory in the workplace is through our interactions with people — by loving and caring for them as Christ did for us.

Here's an example of what giving God the glory in the workplace does not look like.

Ken works in the quality control department at his company. If you sit still long enough you can sometimes hear him snoring from his office. Ken is notoriously lazy, and if you look at the open tabs on his computer browser at work, you will usually see ESPN news or Yahoo! games open. Ken is a pretty nice guy overall, but he is quick to blame the boss when something goes wrong or if a new work policy gets implemented that he doesn't like.

Occasionally, in between gossip emails, Ken will forward his co-workers a "Jesus" email, and around late March every year, you can expect an invitation to Ken's church for the big Easter service. He loves his church and is not afraid to tell everyone about it. Nobody ever comes, but he invites them anyway. Ken's character and actions don't exactly mirror those of the God he allegedly worships.

Though Ken claims to be a Christian, the only way his co-workers know this is from the email forwards and the church invitations.

There is no one-size-fits-all approach to giving glory to God in the workplace, but when we fix our worship on Jesus, our image conforms to his. When we set our minds on Jesus, his character flows out of us into our interactions with employees, employers, and clients.

Rest

"By the seventh day God had finished the work he had been doing; so on the seventh day he rested from all his work." — Genesis 2:2 (NIV)

There comes a time for every artist to lay down the paintbrush and admire the finished product. Once the picture is complete and there is nothing left to paint, the only thing left for the artist to do is to stop working and admire the work.

After God finished creating the universe, he rested, because his work was done. There was nothing left for him to create at that moment; so he sat back and said it was good.

As image-bearers of the Creator, we were designed to live our lives in rhythms of work and rest; just as he did. People were not created to work all the time. Rest is essential to our physical, mental, and emotional well-being. Though God's work was complete after the sixth day, it seems like our work never ends. Monday mornings bring new piles of paperwork, and for many people, the work doesn't go away by Friday afternoon. There is always more work to be done, and for some people, this work cuts into our much-needed times of rest.

According to a study that was published by John Pencavel of Stanford University, productivity in the workplace has proven to drop significantly after a 50-hour workweek. In other words, working longer hours does not necessarily equate to more productivity. The study showed that on average, people who regularly work an 80-hour workweek are no more productive than those who only work 50 hours. Working longer hours has been linked to "absenteeism" and higher employee turnover rates. There are limited seasons where extended work hours could bring more productivity, but these seasons are the exception to the rule.

Whether or not we like to admit it, people need rest. We are wired for it. God desires it for us. Resting is a way for us to admit that we are not God — he is. When we lay our heads on our pillows at night, he does not stop being God. He wants us to depend on him and rest in him. Our need for daily physical rest points to our need for greater spiritual rest. Every morning when we get out of bed, we strive for something. We rest our hope in something, and God wants that something to be him.

"For whoever enters God's rest also rests from his own work, just as God did from His." – Hebrews 4:10 (NIV)

After Jesus had completed the work of atoning for our sins at the cross, he said that it was done; just as he did after his work was done creating the universe. Jesus invited us to rest from our work and our striving to atone for our sins because he already atoned for them. We don't need to work to prove anything to God because when we are hidden in Jesus, we are already everything that we need to be. God doesn't need us to labor for him. He wants us to rest in his labor. God doesn't want your hard work until he first has your rest. He doesn't want your songs until he has your surrender. He isn't impressed with what you can do for him unless it is flowing out of your response to what he has done for you.

One of the greatest mistakes of the church throughout all of history has been focusing on what God wants us to do instead of who God wants us to be. You might feel overwhelmed at times by the desire to do more without having the capacity to sustain it. There are plenty of examples and teachings found in the Scriptures that give reasons why we should be good stewards of our time and resources for the work of the ministry, but there are also many verses about resting and simply "being" (Psalm 46:10, Matthew 11:29).

Taking time out of our week to rest from our work is a way that we can be intentional to remember who we are and who God is. It's a time we can sit with the Father in prayer and meditation without feeling the burden to go and do anything. As we rest in his love and his work, our anxiety and worry are no longer needed because we are already accepted into his family. We are already his children. Out of thankfulness for what he's done, we can examine his character and his actions as we continue to become in practice what he already declared us to be.

Rest is a way of enjoying the fruit of our labor and the fruit of God's labor. It is a time that we should intentionally do something that refreshes our souls. For some people that might be going on a walk in the woods and admiring the work of God's hands. For others, it might be reading an enjoyable book or spending time relaxing with friends. Rest is not something we only do because we are tired; it's something we do because of how we are wired. Being tired is God's reminder to us that he wants us to rest — a reminder that he is God, and we are not.

As someone who works in vocational ministry, there have been times I've felt guilty for slowing down to rest. There are lost people in need of Jesus. And though I do want to be diligent to do my part in fulfilling my calling, I need to remember that God is not waiting on me for anything. I am to wait on God. He commands us to rest, and we should not feel guilty about obeying his command.

Resting means that I stop thinking about my job. It doesn't mean I have a pass to neglect my family or treat my neighbor like trash. It simply means, today I'm not working; I'm not toiling to get things done. Today I am resting and remembering that God is God. On the other hand, it's important to note that resting does not change who we are. Resting from work (even ministry work) does not mean we rest from being ambassadors of Christ. Jesus made it clear in

Mark 3:1-6 that, although we are to rest, it is even more important that we love.

When I take my day off from work, I am still the husband to my wife, the father to my kids, and the worship director at my church. Though I am not actively working, I still treat my family with love and kindness. Resting does not mean that we rest from being God's children; we rest to remember that God did all the work necessary to make us his children. We can rest because we are his children. Our identity does not rest. Our love does not rest (Mark 3:4). And this is the whole point—loving is not something we do. Loving people flows out of us because it is who we are. We can rest to remember that it is not what we do that makes us God's, but it is who we are that controls what we do.

We are made for love, but there is a tension to be held between being and doing. We shouldn't walk away from this chapter thinking that we need to fabricate an appearance of loving people, nor should we walk away thinking that the only thing to do is to sit in solitude while journaling our feelings for Jesus. We must rest in the work of Jesus and drink from his love, knowing that he has done all the work, while considering ways to actively demonstrate this love to others.

The God of the universe, who actively pursues and shows his love for us, is calling each of us into something greater and deeper. May we pause the noise of our busy lives to listen to his voice and see what he is doing. May we rest in his work, work from his rest, and share the joy of his glorious plan with all who will hear.

CHAPTER 10

GATHERED

Potluck

United by Jesus

In the first century, there was a tradition held by the early church where people from every age, race, and socioeconomic status would come together in the name of Jesus to share a meal. This meal was known as the Agape Feast (also known as Love Feast). Despite their many differences, people would come together to be united as brothers and sisters in Christ. The wealthy would bring food to share with the poor, and the slave would sit at the same table with the free. This meal of love and unity was a fragmented picture of heaven on earth as they broke bread and took the cup to remember that it was Christ who united them together by shedding his blood for them on the cross. We know this "remembrance" portion of the tradition today as communion; although, by the third century, communion and love feasts became two separate things. And while the sacrament of communion is still practiced by many churches today, love feasts are not as common as they once were.

In a lot of ways, the Agape Feast symbolized all of life as it should be. There was no Jew or Greek, man or woman, slave or free. All people came together to be united under the name and provision of Jesus Christ, serving and loving one another as they remembered and thanked Jesus for the way that he served and loved them. Every time the church takes communion, we are remembering that we are united, not only with Jesus but also with each and every believer in churches all over the world. Jesus is the bread that fills and unites us, bringing people from every tribe, tongue, and nation together in thankful remembrance. Though our communion and love feasts on this earth are imperfect, they serve as a picture of the perfect unity that is to come.

This gathering together of God's people is a snapshot of the narrative found throughout the whole Bible. Genesis begins with a family that communes with God, and Revelation concludes with one giant family doing the same. When the church gathers together in the name of Jesus, to eat from his Word and drink from his love, it is a picture of what heaven will be like. (Ezekiel 34:13, Isaiah 11:12, Zephaniah 3:20, Psalm 106:47, Amos 9:14, Matthew 24:31, Revelation 21:1-3)

We were made to be part of a family. We need community. Our purpose depends on it. Throughout all of history, God has been assembling people together to form something bigger than ourselves. In Luke 15, Jesus tells the parable of the lost sheep. A shepherd with a hundred sheep loses one of his sheep; so, he leaves the ninety-nine to go after the one. This parable is signifying God's relentless love and value for each individual person. This isn't like losing one dollar when you have ninety-nine more; it's more like losing one of your children. Regardless of how many children you have, there is no acceptable loss when one is missing. Each individual has intrinsic value as a human being and is loved by God.

"...there is rejoicing in the presence of the angels of God over one sinner who repents." – Luke 15:10 (NIV)

Though God greatly loves the lost sheep, his desire is that it returns to the fold with the other sheep. His love for the sheep leads him on a rescue mission to retrieve it. Being part of a family does not lessen the worth of the individual; it multiplies it.

Let me illustrate it like this.

If you've ever spent time putting a puzzle together, then you know that the ultimate goal is a finished picture. We could say that the ultimate glory of the puzzle is when the picture is complete. Humans are like puzzle pieces. Each puzzle piece is significant and serves a unique role in the big picture. The purpose of the puzzle piece is to serve the entire puzzle for the sake of its completion. A puzzle piece with no puzzle would be essentially meaningless. It would be discarded because it no longer served a purpose. However, in the context of the completed puzzle, a single piece has more value than if it were by itself. And if a single piece were missing, it would be worth tearing the whole house apart just to find it (Luke 15:8). In the story of the lost sheep, Jesus was making a case for the value of one person; just like the value of a single puzzle piece to the whole puzzle. But God is building something bigger than a puzzle.

"You also, like living stones, are being built into a spiritual house to be a holy priesthood, offering spiritual sacrifices acceptable to God through Jesus Christ." – 1 Peter 2:5 (NIV)

God is building a temple, a dwelling place for himself, made of living stones; and we are the stones. The people of the church are the pieces to the temple, and Jesus is the foundational cornerstone. The individual stones need the temple, and the temple needs the stones. It is a symbiotic relationship; just like the one between a puzzle and its pieces. We are images that were designed to complete a bigger image. We were designed for a purpose and we were given a command to obey. The two are one and the same. Our purpose and Christ's command to us is that we love one another. It would be an impossible task to love without involving others. We could not love our neighbor without our neighbor. We could not serve one another without one another. Love is not just giving generously; it is giving generously for the gain of someone else. Love must include others. Fulfilling God's first words to humanity to be fruitful and multiply is only possible in community. Multiplication cannot happen in isolation. And as people who were made in the image of God, we are not complete on our own.

Paul the Apostle often illustrated this concept with the imagery of a body with its different body parts.

"Just as a body, though one, has many parts, but all its many parts form one body, so it is with Christ." – 1 Corinthians 12:12 (NIV)

A person is like a single body part. Though a hand by itself is a complete hand, it is much more useful when it is connected to the rest of the body than when it is by itself. Though the church body is made of many parts with different functions, we are all one body. And when the body comes together, we can live out our purpose in a way that we cannot do alone. For a body to be joined together, there must be agreement. There must be unity. A leg that is not in agreement with the mind is crippled. An eye that is not in agreement with the rest of the body is blind. Though we are all flawed, there is a unifying agent that aligns and brings us together, and his name is Jesus. When we look to Jesus, we see the perfect human. And it's in beholding him that we become like him; both as individuals and as a collective body. Jesus demonstrated love by laying down his life for all, not just for his friends but also for his enemies. Our differences and preferences will never be more important than our unity. But it's only in the examining of and conforming to Jesus' likeness that we will be able to come together in complete oneness.

One of the most emphasized themes in the letters to the early church was the theme of unity. Over the years, the church has allowed all things big and small to cause division. Even things that were meant to be unifying such as love feasts and corporate worship gatherings have still become objects of division. The propensity to divide over an issue or a preference is not new to modern Christianity. It has always been in our nature to look at our own needs before looking at the needs of others. And while there is nothing wrong with having individual needs or wants, we are not called to pursue these things but to lay them down. We are called to love, and "love is not self-seeking" (1 Corinthians 13: 5).

In this season of the Covid-19 pandemic, I've seen the church-at-large divide over various things such as political stances and mask-wearing policies. While it would be nice to go to the Scriptures for the answers to our questions, sometimes, the answers we find don't appear as black and white as we'd like. One church might strongly object to any government-imposed mandates while the church down the street is on the opposite side of that same issue. Both churches could be looking at the same issue with an identical goal in mind but have differences in their approach. One church might say that the most loving thing to do for their members is to cancel all services until it is safe to be in person. Another church might say that the most loving thing to do for their members is to continue meeting in person for the sake of nurturing spiritual health during a time of isolation. Which church is right, and which is wrong?

It's easy to make a claim that says this or that is the most loving thing to do; but what about the unity which we were called? While it may not always be clear in God's Word whether one action is more loving than the other, it is clear that we are to strive to keep unity.

"Make every effort to keep the unity of the Spirit through the bond of peace." – Ephesians 4:3 (NIV)

While social media gives disagreeable people more courage than ever to speak their minds, there is something much greater at risk than being wrong about a social or political issue. If an arm is broken, the rest of the body can care for it and help it to heal. Or if the knee gets scratched, the hands can clean it and wrap it with bandages. But if each of the body parts inflicts pain on the others, then self-destruction is looming, and healing is impossible. There will always be issues that come with a choice to unite or divide, and it's how we deal with those issues that will expose who or what we are worshiping. When we worship Jesus, we will lay down our very lives to bring unity; because that's what Jesus did for us.

What if we were slow to speak and quick to listen in a disagreement? What if we spoke with honor to one another in our differences instead of speaking with condescension? What if we sacrificed our comfort and preferences for the sake of someone else's comfort and preferences? We cannot look to Jesus and walk away thinking it's acceptable to "cancel" someone who disagrees with us. Though Jesus never shied away from speaking the truth, he also never shied away from speaking it in love. While it may come easy for some people to drop truth bombs, it's probably worth considering the fact that most people don't enjoy having bombs dropped on them. People like to be treated with respect and dignity. And being made in the image of God has given all people the right to be treated as such. This includes the people we disagree with. We can disagree without dividing. Because when God disagreed with us, he sent Jesus to be a bridge back to him. When we worship the God of second chances — the God of patience and kindness — we, too, will be transformed into creatures who build bridges instead of walls. Jesus is the one who unites us with God, and when his Spirit is in us, we will strive for unity with others.

All things for building up

The God who created the world is still creating in the world today. He is creating and recreating, building and rebuilding. Sometimes buildings need to be torn down so they can be rebuilt again. And when it comes to the family of God, this is exactly what Jesus did. He was the temple that was torn down on our behalf so that we could be the temple to be raised to life again. Jesus was condemned for us so that we could be restored anew. Three days after Jesus' lifeless body lay in the grave, the Spirit raised him from the dead. From that moment, he began construction on the new temple — the church.

"Jesus answered them, "Destroy this temple, and I will raise it again in three days." — John 2:19 (ESV)

Christ is building his church, and so should we. The purpose of all humanity both individually and collectively is to drink from the living water of Jesus and to lock arms with those around us in love as we build each other up. This is why the church comes together — to remind each other of the love of God and spur one another on in obedience and purpose.

"What then shall we say, brothers and sisters? When you come together, each of you has a hymn, or a word of instruction, a revelation, a tongue or an interpretation. Everything must be done so that the church may be built up." — *1 Corinthians 14:26 (ESV)*

In a day and age where consumerism has invaded society at every turn, where every holiday has become commercialized, and slogans like, "Have it your way" have pervaded the way we choose our social environments, the church is not immune. "Church shopping" is a common term used for finding a pastor who is funny yet doctrinally sound, or for finding a worship style that suits our preference of traditional or modern. We've been trained to view everything as a commodity, but there is one major problem with this. Though it is important that we are in a community that is aligned with the teachings of the Scriptures, I'm afraid the consumeristic approach causes us to treat the church as a means of fulfilling our needs without considering the needs of others. This mindset inherently makes us think about ourselves more than our neighbors. But the church does not gather primarily to get. We gather to give. We gather to love one another, serve one another, bear one another's burdens, and build each other up in the commands of Christ.

Attending a church service without interacting with the people is a little like going to a gym without working out. I am not trying to minimize the importance of hearing from God's Word, but even listening to a sermon is something we can all do from our devices in private. Hearing from God's Word is imperative, but the purpose of the gathering is to build up the body. Building is active, not passive.

One of the greatest challenges for the church during the Covid-19 pandemic was that the church was not able to meet for the better half of the year due to mandated social-distancing and safety precautions. Many evangelical churches moved weekly services to be an online program with no physical gathering. While the idea of online services was in the best interest of the church, it presented challenges for the church to be in community with one another. Though the church is not a building, the church is also not a service or a program. The church is a body of believers, and the body must be built up.

Every part of the body is needed for it to be healthy and effective, and when one part is missing, the rest of the body suffers. We need to be committed to finding our role in the body. We are not all teachers or worship leaders, but we all have a unique calling for building up the church. That calling may or may not be an official position. Consider these examples.

Mike sits in the same place every week. I know when Mike is there or not during worship; because when he is there, everyone around him catches his fire. Mike is not an official worship leader at our church, but he leads worship from his chair every week. He sings with so much passion, and he is right there with us every step of the way. His hands are the first to be raised during a song, and if he agrees with something during a service, he's going to let everyone around him know it. Mike is a charismatic worshiper, and his joyful charisma is contagious. I love leading worship when Mike is in the room. Oftentimes after a church service, Mike will make his way to the front to shake my hand and tell me how thankful he is for my leadership and how much our time of worship blessed him. Mike may have no idea how thankful I am, as a worship leader, to him as well. Mike's role is not an official serve position at our church, but it is no less important for building up the worship team.

Lori also serves the worship team in an unofficial capacity. She bakes goodies and writes notes of encouragement for the band and leaves them in the green room each week. Lori is happy to serve in more of a behind-the-scenes role. She doesn't expect any accolades or rewards, but she is a faithful encourager and builds up the worship team in meaningful ways. Her smile and thankful sincerity, along with her notes and food, create a warm atmosphere for the worship team to feel loved and important. This may seem like a little thing to some people, but to the band, this is more than meaningful. She is building up the people who stand on the stage to build up everyone else.

Mike and Lori have identified their roles in serving the body through ways that are unique to their giftings. And this is what each of us is called to do. As Paul said in 1 Corinthians 3:6, one person plants a seed, another person waters, and God gives the increase. We each have a part, and without every part, we are like a hand that is missing a finger or a leg that is missing a foot. A body part that is detached from the rest of the body is a dead body part. Its only future is decay. But when the body comes together, we can remind each other of the love of God while demonstrating it to each other. We can point each other to the patience of God as we are patient with one another. We speak the hope of God's love to one another in the midst of our challenging times. And we stir one another up to walk in our purpose.

"And let us consider how to stir up one another to love and good works, not neglecting to meet together, as is the habit of some, but encouraging one another, and all the more as you see the Day drawing near." – Hebrews 10:24-25 (ESV)

As we learn more knowledge about God and his character, it leads us into a deeper love and devotion towards him. This same principle is true of loving others. When I first met my wife, I knew little about her. The more time that I spent with her, the more knowledge I gained. I learned about her likes and dislikes, her experiences and personal preferences. I heard her tell stories about times of grief and times of joy. I learned about her family dynamics and her friends, what her school was like and what kind of food she liked to eat. All this knowledge led me to a deeper love for her. And the more time I spent with her, the more I learned. Still today, the more I learn about her, the more I love and care for her. If we are to stir one another up to love and good works, then we should consider that love is a response to time spent with someone. My introverted nature is tempted to retreat and isolate after a church service, but I know that when I speak to people, I learn more about them and find out ways that I can love and serve them better. There are people at my church who have almost nothing in common with me other than their love for Jesus. But I've learned that when I hear them talk about their passions and interests, my understanding of these people increases, and I can form a unique bond with them.

Many times, our lack of empathy towards the plight of someone else's life is simply a result of lacking understanding. It's in knowing that Jesus laid down his life for all people that leads us to lay down our desires to isolate from people who are different from us. But engaging in the stories of people who are different from us is one of the most valuable things we can do to build up the body. Learning our differences is one of the best ways to learn how to bridge our differences together. Learning the struggle of someone else is one of the best ways to grow in our empathy for that person. The relationships and conversations that happen between believers at church gatherings are significant for growing in our love for one another. When we are filled with the love and the light of Jesus, it will shine out of us and touch our brothers and sisters. Who in your church small group are you getting to know deeply with the sole purpose of loving them? Who are you getting to know that is different from you so that you can grow in your compassion for them?

"Anyone who loves their brother and sister lives in the light, and there is nothing in them to make them stumble." – 1 John 2:10 (NIV)

It's difficult to love someone well that we don't know. We can show kindness and compassion to a stranger, but how will we know their needs? The reason that Jesus was able to love us more than anyone else ever could is that he knows every single thing about us. He knows the number of hairs on your head and he knows every thought you have ever thought (Luke 12:7). If the greatest command is that we love our neighbor as ourselves, then shouldn't we get to know our neighbors? Shouldn't we get to know the poor and the oppressed? How can we empathize with someone who is hurting when we are unwilling to be around people who do not look like us? It may sound like a burden too great to carry to love all the homeless people in your city, but what if you were able to show the love of God to just one? What if every child of God loved one person the way that Christ loves us? What kind of impact would this have on fatherlessness, poverty, and crime in your city?

As the church continues to rise up, bringing signs of the kingdom to our communities, pouring out the love and justice of God that fills us, we hold to the hope that one day the kingdom of God will rule and reign on this earth. And his reign will be one of peace on earth forever.

"Of the greatness of his government and peace there will be no end. He will reign on David's throne and over his kingdom, establishing and upholding it with justice and righteousness from that time on and forever..." — Isaiah 9:7 (NIV)

CLOSING THOUGHTS

God's desire for you to worship him is rooted in his love for you. He wants what is best for you, and that is to be fully who God made you to be. Worship is not just something you do on the weekend; it's something you do every day. You can take an inventory of your worship by considering your desires, thoughts, words, and actions. Where do your time and money go? Who or what gets your best? What are you working towards? What image are you becoming? Consider your purpose to love God with your heart, soul, and mind; and to love your neighbor as yourself. Your purpose is bound up in your relationships with God and with people, and it is realized through worship.

If your purpose relies on your relationship with God, then you must cultivate your relationship with him. Treat feeding your soul, by meditating on God's love and his Word, in the same way that you feed your belly. Do not go without it. In a day of CrossFit workouts and Keto diets, the phrase "You get out what you put in" is not a foreign concept. We should expect to see the success of our results based on the amount of effort we put in. If we cheat on diets every other meal, then we should not expect to see drastic changes in our vitality. If we work out once per month, we should not expect to see chiseled abs. God does all the work, but we must actively rest in him. He is the living water, but we must come to the well and drink. He is sovereign, but we are responsible.

Be intentional to let the love of Jesus in, and be just as intentional and disciplined to let it come out. Start right now as you set this book down. Show your love for your spouse, your sibling, your friend, and your neighbor. Consider God's sacrificial love for you and then go and make a sacrifice for someone else.

How can you leverage your entire life for the gospel? Not just by doing more activity, but by loving people more. Let every situation be informed by the question, "What would Jesus do?" Because that is what he wants you to image. The love of Jesus must be the fuel for our worship, or we will simply turn "loving" into a burden to carry instead of a response of thankfulness to what he has done for us. You are what you worship, and God says you are his child. Go and sin no more. Choose this day who you will serve — who you will obey and worship. Go and be who God has declared you to be. Go and live out your purpose. Behold him and become!

BIBLIOGRAPHY

Batura, Paul, *Changing the World Through Adoption*, March 2017 https://jimdaly.focusonthefamily.com/improbable-adoption-story-steve-jobs/

Best, Harold *Unceasing Worship: Biblical Perspectives on Worship and the Arts,* InterVarsity Publishing 2003

Daly, Jim *Focus on the Family Broadcast*, March 2017

DeRouchie, Jason *Love God with Your Everything,* Desiring God, 2013 https://www.desiringgod.org/articles/love-god-with-your-everything

Dumas, Alexandre *The Count of Monte Cristo,* Signet Classics Publishing 2005

Jordan, Tom "No Winter Sun? Norwegian Mountain Town Installs Giant Mirrors," CNN. November 2013 https://www.cnn.com/travel/article/rjukan-sun-mirror/index.html

Keller, Timothy *The Reason for God: Belief in an Age of Skepticism,* Dutton 2008

Knight, Kevin *Synod of Laodicea (4th Century) New Advent* http://www.newadvent.org/fathers/3806.htm

Lewis, C.S. *Mere Christianity,* Geoffrey Bles Publishing, 1952

Lewis, C.S. *The Lion, the Witch and the Wardrobe,* Geoffrey Bles Publishing, October 1950

Lerner, Jennifer S. **Li,** Ye **Valdesolo,** Piercarlo **Kassam,** Karim *Emotion and Decision-Making,* Annual Review of Psychology, June 2014 https://scholar.harvard.edu/files/jenniferlerner/files/annual_review_manuscript_june_16_final.final_.pdf

Mannes, Elena *The Power of Music: Pioneering Discoveries in the New Science of Song,* Walker Publishing, 2011

Merton, Thomas *The Seven Storey Mountain,* Harcourt Publishing, 1948

National Center for Educational Services https://nces.ed.gov/fastfacts/display.asp?id=372#:~:text=About%203.7%20million%20students%20are,from%20private%20schools%20(source)

Percival, Henry *Nicene and Post-Nicene Fathers, Second Series, Vol. 14. Edited by Philip Schaff and Henry Wace*, Buffalo, NY: Christian Literature Publishing Co., 1900

Peterson, Merrill D. *Lincoln in American Memory*. New York and Oxford: Oxford University Press, 1995.

Robinson, Sarah Bring Back the 40-hour Work Week 2012 https://www.salon.com/2012/03/14/bring_back_the_40_hour_work_week/

Saint Augustine, *The Confessions of St. Augustine*, Create Space Publishing 2014

Spurgeon, Charles *Christian Classics Collection*, Niche Edition 2011

Temple, William *Nature, Man, and God*, Kessinger Publishing 2003

Mag

Topical

Ask a person

Digging Deeper ?
Template

Starting Point
— Grace

4th Bible Project videos

Prayer + fasting

Healing

Made in the USA
Columbia, SC
07 March 2021